The Brooks Range

ALASKA GEOGRAPHIC

Vol. 23, No. 3 / 1996

EDITOR
Penny Rennick

PRODUCTION DIRECTOR
Kathy Doogan

MARKETING MANAGER
Pattey Parker Mancini

CIRCULATION/DATABASE MANAGER
Linda Flowers

BOARD OF DIRECTORS
Richard Carlson
Kathy Doogan
Penny Rennick

Robert A. Henning, PRESIDENT EMERITUS

POSTMASTER: Send address changes to:

ALASKA GEOGRAPHIC®
P.O. Box 93370
Anchorage, Alaska 99509-3370

PRINTED IN U.S.A.

ISBN: 1-56661-032-X

Price to non-members this issue: $19.95

COLOR SEPARATIONS: Graphic Chromatics

PRINTING: The Hart Press

COVER: *A kettle pond reflects an image of the Endicott Mountains. (Patrick J. Endres)*

PREVIOUS PAGE: *Rafters tackle Kobuk River rapids below Walker Lake. (Chlaus Lotscher)*

FACING PAGE: *The Arrigetch Peaks create a throne fit for a mountain king in the central Brooks Range. (George Wuerthner)*

ALASKA GEOGRAPHIC® (ISSN 0361-1353) is published quarterly by The Alaska Geographic Society, 639 West International Airport Rd., Unit 38, Anchorage, AK 99518. Periodicals postage paid at Anchorage, Alaska, and additional mailing offices. Copyright © 1996 by The Alaska Geographic Society. All rights reserved. Registered trademark: Alaska Geographic, ISSN 0361-1353; Key title Alaska Geographic.

THE ALASKA GEOGRAPHIC SOCIETY is a non-profit, educational organization dedicated to improving geographic understanding of Alaska and the North, putting geography back in the classroom and exploring new methods of teaching and learning.

MEMBERS RECEIVE *ALASKA GEOGRAPHIC*®, a high-quality, colorful quarterly that devotes each issue to monographic, in-depth coverage of a northern region or resource-oriented subject. Back issues are also available. For current membership rates, or to order or request a free catalog of back issues, contact: The Alaska Geographic Society, P.O. Box 93370, Anchorage, AK 99509-3370; phone (907) 562-0164, fax (907) 562-0479, e-mail: akgeo@anc.ak.net.

SUBMITTING PHOTOGRAPHS: Those interested in submitting photographs should write for a list of future topics or other specific photo needs and a copy of our editorial guidelines. We cannot be responsible for unsolicited submissions. Submissions not accompanied by sufficient postage for return by certified mail will be returned by regular mail.

CHANGE OF ADDRESS: The post office does not automatically forward *ALASKA GEOGRAPHIC*® when you move. To ensure continuous service, please notify us at least six weeks before moving. Send your new address and membership number or a mailing label from a recent *ALASKA GEOGRAPHIC*® to: The Alaska Geographic Society, Box 93370, Anchorage, AK 99509. If your book is returned to us by the post office, we will contact you to ask if you wish to receive a replacement for $5 (to cover postage costs).

The Library of Congress has cataloged this serial publication as follows:

Alaska Geographic. v.1-
[Anchorage, Alaska Geographic Society] 1972-
v. ill. (part col.). 23 x 31 cm.
Quarterly
Official publication of The Alaska Geographic Society.
Key title: Alaska geographic, ISSN 0361-1353.

1. Alaska—Description and travel—1959-
—Periodicals. I. Alaska Geographic Society.

F901.A266   917.98′04′505   72-92087

Library of Congress 75[79112] MARC-S.

ABOUT THIS ISSUE: Gil Mull, a former U.S. Geological Survey and current state Division of Geological and Geophysical Surveys geologist, has been exploring the Brooks Range for more than three decades. He shares his intimate knowledge of Alaska's northern rampart in "Mystic Mountains." Writer and teacher Nick Jans has been living within the shadow of the Brooks Range at Ambler for several years. As a year-round resident of Brooks Range country, he has many adventures to share with readers, including the account in this issue of "The Perfect Loop." Jans is the author of *Last Light Breaking* (1994) and *A Place Beyond* (1996). Anthropologist Chris Wooley, of Anchorage, is a former resident of Barrow and has worked with the Inupiat people of the North Slope. He is currently preparing a detailed study of the Nunamiut of Anaktuvuk Pass for the National Park Service and is the author of "Alaska's Arctic Mountain People" in this issue. Penny Rennick is the editor of *ALASKA GEOGRAPHIC*®.

Several Alaskans helped with research and checked portions of the manuscript. We thank Wendy Davis of the National Park Service in Anchorage; Jeff Mow and Glen A. Dodson of Gates of the Arctic National Park; Bob Gerhard, formerly with the Northwest Region national parks in Kotzebue and now in Anchorage; Kim Valentino, chief of education and interpretation for the Northwest Region; Jack Mosby with the National Park Service's Rivers, Trails, and Conservation Assistance Program; Nancy Tileston with the U.S. Fish and Wildlife Service in Anchorage; and Janet Jorgenson and Pat Reynolds with the Arctic National Wildlife Refuge in Fairbanks. We thank John Favro with Tongass National Forest for help with the Tracy Arm article in the *ALASKA GEOGRAPHIC*® Newsletter.

Population figures are from the State of Alaska, Department of Community and Regional Affairs. Figures for mountain elevations are from the *Dictionary of Alaska Place Names* (1971) by Donald Orth with the exception of Mount Sukakpak.

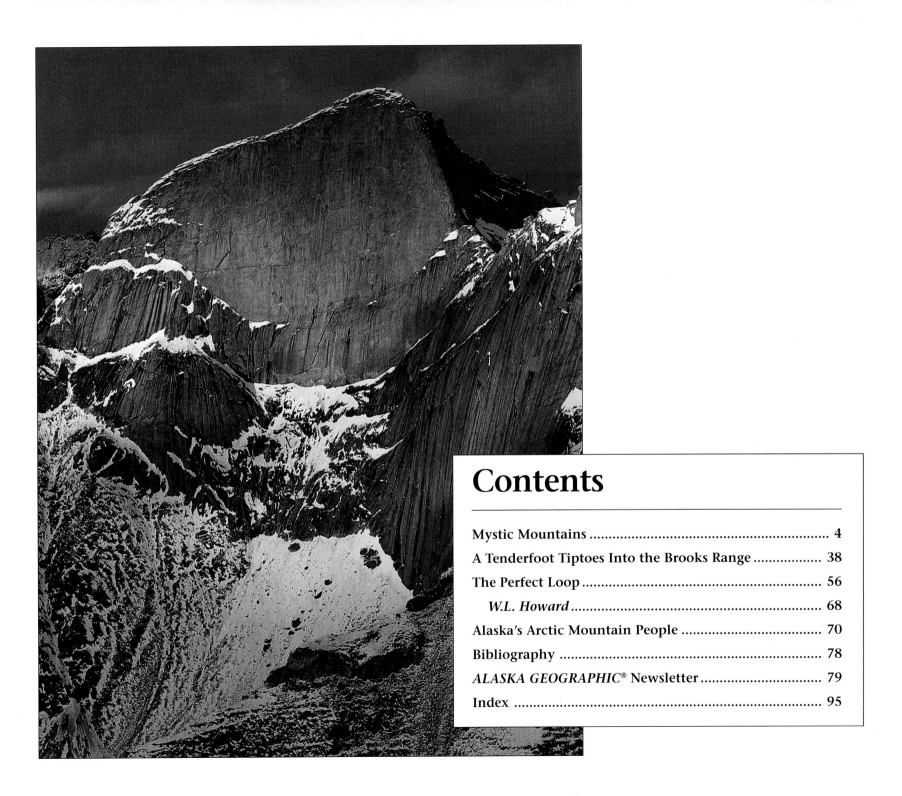

Contents

Mystic Mountains

By Gil Mull

The Brooks Range offers an extremely diverse suite of terrain features throughout its 720-mile length, but it is united by a common geological thread; this thread, which is its geologic history and evolution, gives the Brooks Range a distinctive character that differs markedly from most of the other mountain ranges in Alaska. Part of the fascination of the Brooks Range is its remoteness and wilderness, whether or not all of it meets the official definition of the term. The range is everywhere interesting, and in places is truly spectacular. Although this wilderness is not to be taken lightly at any time of year, generally the Brooks Range can be considered a friendly wilderness in which during the summer most areas can be relatively easily crossed by experienced hikers or boaters. In contrast, long foot or boat traverses in most of the other mountain ranges in Alaska are feasible only for the most highly skilled wilderness travelers and mountaineers. Many of the highest peaks in the Brooks Range are remote and require long cross-country travel for access, but only a few are of such height or technical difficulty as to be considered major mountaineering objectives. However, the range abounds with lower-elevation vertical limestone and, in some places, granite cliffs with technical climbing routes that in more accessible areas would attract numerous climbers.

An understanding of the way the rocks in

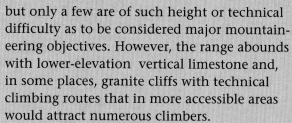

LEFT: *Wildflowers crown a bluff near Cape Lisburne where the Brooks Range tumbles into the Chukchi Sea. (Gil Mull)*

FACING PAGE: *Hikers enjoy this view overlooking the Killik River on the north side of the Brooks Range. Rivers flowing north out of the central Brooks Range like the Killik drain into the Colville River that empties into the Arctic Ocean. These rivers receive less river traffic, in part because access to and from the rivers is difficult and costly. (Chlaus Lotscher)*

*In this clear altitude, where the basic forces of the
earth are building, it seems absurd to reckon time
in human years. The scrubby plants are scarce
more momentary than men who pass in transitory
generations, leaving no more trace than does a fly
on the steady hand of a craftsman at his labour.*

—Freya Stark

The Brooks Range

(© 1996 Alaska Geographic Society; map by Kathy Doogan)

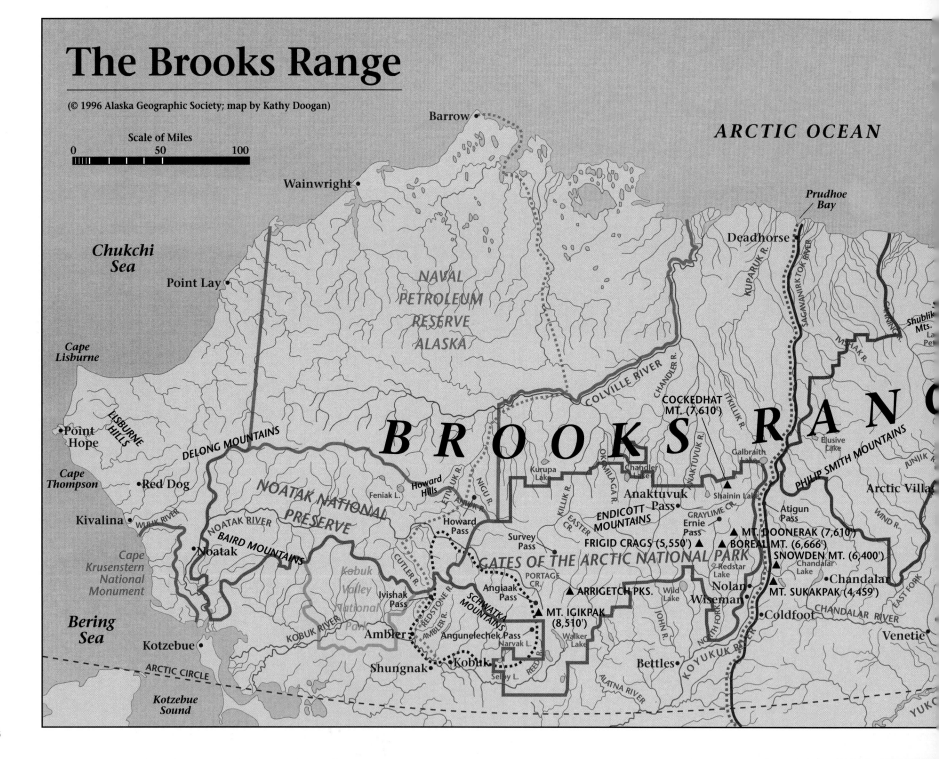

Scale of Miles

0   50   100

ARCTIC OCEAN

Barrow

Wainwright

Chukchi Sea

Point Lay

Prudhoe Bay

Deadhorse

NAVAL PETROLEUM RESERVE ALASKA

Cape Lisburne

KUPARUK R.

SAGAVANIRKTOK RIVER

Shublik Mts.

COLVILLE RIVER

CHANDLER R.

COCKEDHAT MT. (7,610')

ITKILLIK R.

Elusive Lake

B R O O K S   R A N G

PHILIP SMITH MOUNTAINS

LISBURNE HILLS

Point Hope

DELONG MOUNTAINS

Kurupa Lake

OKPILAK R.

OMILAGA R.

NAKTUVUK R.

Galbraith

Cape Thompson

Red Dog

Feniak L.

Howard Hills

Howard Hills

ETIVLUK R.

NIGU R.

AIYUK R.

Chandler Lake

Shainin Lake

Arctic Villa

Kivalina

WULIK RIVER

NOATAK NATIONAL PRESERVE

Anaktuvuk Pass

KILLIK R.

EASTER CR.

ENDICOTT MOUNTAINS

GRAYLIME CR.

Atigun Pass

JUNJIK R.

WIND R.

NOATAK RIVER

Howard Pass

Survey Pass

Ernie Pass

FRIGID CRAGS (5,550') ▲

▲ MT. DOONERAK (7,610')

Cape Krusenstern National Monument

BAIRD MOUNTAINS

Noatak

CUTLER R.

Kobuk Valley National Park

GATES OF THE ARCTIC NATIONAL PARK

▲ BOREAL MT. (6,666')

SNOWDEN MT. (6,400') ▲

PORTAGE CR.

Redstar Lake

Chandalar Lake

Kotzebue

KOBUK RIVER

Ivishak Pass

REDSTONE R.

Angiaak Pass

▲ ARRIGETCH PKS.

Wild Lake

Nolan

Wiseman

▲

MT. SUKAKPAK (4,459')

Chandalar

Bering Sea

AMBLER R.

SCHWATKA MOUNTAINS

▲ MT. IGIKPAK (8,510')

JOHN R.

Venetie

Ambler

Angunelechek Pass

Narvak L.

Walker Lake

CHANDALAR RIVER

Kotzebue

Shungnak

Kobuk

Selby L.

REED R.

NORTH FORK

Bettles

KOYUKUK RIVER

Coldfoot

EAST FORK

ALATNA RIVER

ARCTIC CIRCLE

Kotzebue Sound

YUKO

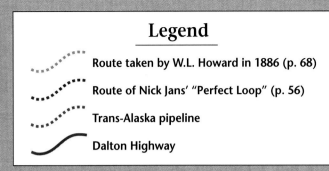

Legend

······ Route taken by W.L. Howard in 1886 (p. 68)

•••••• Route of Nick Jans' "Perfect Loop" (p. 56)

•••••• Trans-Alaska pipeline

〰️ Dalton Highway

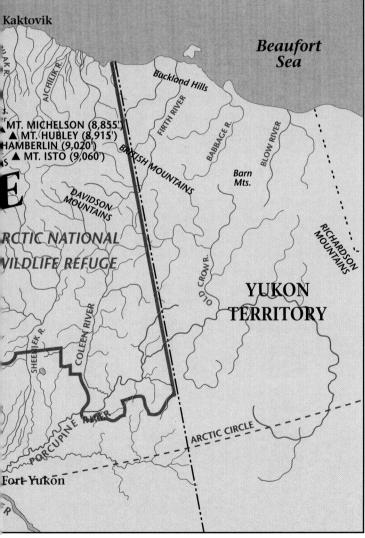

the Brooks Range were deposited and deformed adds greatly to the appreciation of its uniqueness, and may also simplify route selection in wilderness journeys. The range is composed primarily of layered sedimentary rocks, some of which date from the early Paleozoic era back into the Precambrian, more than 570 million years ago. A few areas of dark-colored layered volcanic rocks are also present. Most of these sedimentary and volcanic rocks were deposited during the Paleozoic era, between 220 and 370 million years ago, and throughout most of the range have been uplifted, faulted and in some places intensely folded. Some of the rocks have been altered and recrystallized by heat and pressure to form metamorphic rocks, and, in addition, some areas of granitic rocks are found in the heart of the range. These coarse-grained igneous rocks were formed as molten rock intruded upward into the overlying sedimentary rocks, where it cooled slowly to form uniform light-colored masses of rock that in some places have been sculptured into towering smooth cliffs without visible layering. Collectively, the granitic and Paleozoic sedimentary rocks are relatively resistant and form the highest, most rugged and most spectacular scenic portions of the range.

Most of the foothills on the north side of the Brooks Range are underlain by sedimentary rocks of Mesozoic age — the age of the dinosaurs, which ranges from 66 million years to about 220 million years ago. These rocks consist primarily of alternating sandstone and shale horizons that, in contrast with the mountains, are relatively nonresistant and form the more subdued rolling tundra-covered Arctic Foothills belt of the Arctic Slope, which grades almost imperceptibly into the Arctic Coastal Plain that flanks the Beaufort and Chukchi seas. These Mesozoic rocks also occur in a few infolds within the range, where they form isolated Shangri-Lalike areas of subdued topography surrounded by rugged mountain peaks.

Many of the late Precambrian and early Paleozoic rocks that are now exposed in the Brooks Range are relatively fine-grained muds that were deposited as shale and later compacted to form argillite. In other areas, carbonate and volcanic rocks were also deposited in ocean basins far from land. About 385 million years ago, in the middle of the Devonian period, these ocean basins were compressed and uplifted into a major mountain range that extended over most of northern Alaska — a predecessor to the present Brooks Range. From this mountain range, thousands of feet of sand and gravel were deposited and later compacted to form the Kanayut conglomerate, which now underlies large areas of the crest of the central Brooks Range.

By early Mississippian time, about 360 million years ago, this large mountain range was reduced by erosion to a nearly flat plain with a few low hills at the edge of a large continent that lay to the north, in the area of the present North Slope and Beaufort Sea. During the Mississippian and Pennsylvanian periods, a duration of about 45 million years, sea level slowly rose and much of northern

BELOW RIGHT: *Several species of mammals occur throughout the Brooks Range, but this northern environment demands that they maintain large territories to feed themselves. It is possible to see grizzly bear, caribou, moose, Dall sheep, wolf and numerous smaller mammals, but visitors should be meticulous about storing food properly and leaving a clean campsite. This bear has found human garbage left by careless travelers on the Dalton Highway at Atigun Pass. (Ron Wendt)*

BELOW: *Narvak Lake and neighboring Selby Lake lie west of the Angayucham Mountains on the north side of the Kobuk River in Gates of the Arctic National Preserve. (George Wuerthner)*

LEFT: *Vegetation in the Brooks Range may look rather scant but a closer look reveals an abundance of nourishing plants. This patch contains lowbush cranberries in fruit and plentiful bearberry. (Jon R. Nickles)*

BELOW: *Outcrops of shale mark the slopes of Kuyuktuvuk Creek valley in the Endicott Mountains. The creek flows 14 1/2 miles to join the Dietrich River near 6,400-foot Snowden Mountain. (Jon R. Nickles)*

Alaska was covered by a warm, shallow sea in which corals and other marine organisms flourished. Light-colored limestone and dolomite known as the Lisburne limestone were deposited up to 2,000 feet in depth, and now form many areas of spectacular light gray cliffs and mountains in much of the northern part of the Brooks Range. During this time, the shoreline lay generally along the trend of the present arctic coastline, but with the important difference that the land lay to the north.

During the late Pennsylvanian and part of the Permian periods, about 250 to 330 million years ago, the shoreline moved slowly southward as sea level dropped, possibly as a result of the large amounts of water tied up in vast glaciers in the Southern Hemisphere. When sea level rose again, thin sandstone and shale were deposited over the dead carbonate banks until the Triassic period, about 245 million years ago, when a gentle uplift of the land to the north occurred. From this uplift, a series of sediment-loaded, braided streams spread a blanket of up to 400 feet of sand and gravel southward, and

LEFT: *Mollie Matteson gathers blueberries in the Hammond River valley in Gates of the Arctic National Park. Visitors are allowed to pick berries, mushrooms and other vegetation for their own use while in the park, but they are not allowed to harvest natural resources for export outside the park. (George Wuerthner)*

BELOW: *These fossil pelecypods were found in the Lisburne limestone of the northeastern Brooks Range. Pelecypods are members of a class of bivalve mollusks such as clams, oysters and mussels that have a bilaterally symmetrical body encased in a shell connected by a hinge at the animal's back. (Arne Bakke)*

Shoreline along the confluence of the North Fork of the Koyukuk and Bonanza Creek provides an ideal setting for this camp. The North Fork is one of several designated Wild and Scenic Rivers flowing out of the Brooks Range. (Jon R. Nickles)

A hiker looks into the Philip Smith Mountains from Atigun Canyon on the Dalton Highway. Philip Smith (1877-1949) was Chief Alaskan Geologist for the U.S. Geological Survey from 1924 to 1946 and pioneered routes in the Alatna, Koyukuk, Kobuk and Noatak drainages. (Patrick J. Endres)

formed the Sadlerochit Formation. In the northeastern Brooks Range, these rocks form a conspicuous reddish-brown-weathering cap above the gray Lisburne limestone. In the subsurface of the North Slope, they form the major reservoir at the Prudhoe Bay oil field.

From the late Triassic into the Jurassic period, marine deposition prevailed in northern Alaska, and a layer of silt and mud was deposited on a gently south-sloping shelf. However, near the middle of the Jurassic period, about 180 million years ago, a profound geologic event began to affect northern Alaska as the result of the collision of two pieces of the earth's crust, or lithosphere. The compression from the collision resulted in the uplift of a large pile of the crust in much the same fashion as a snowplow or large bulldozer piles up material in front of its advancing blade. In northern Alaska, the blade of the plow appears to have been a piece of oceanic crust — crust typical of that found in deep ocean basins — that began to override and scrape up the edge of the continental crust on which the Kanayut, Lisburne, Sadlerochit and other sedimentary rocks in northern Alaska had been deposited. This collision continued for about 60 million years and formed what we now know as the Brooks Range.

In the process, volcanic rocks of the oceanic crust were also uplifted and are preserved as remnants that form the southern flank of the Brooks Range. The area of convergence between crustal plates is commonly known as a subduction zone. In most subduction zones, one plate of oceanic crust is overridden by another piece of oceanic crust or by a piece of relatively light continental crust. But in the case of the Brooks Range, for reasons not clearly understood, the relatively light continental rocks were overridden by the dense oceanic rocks; this is a special case of subduction known as obduction. Evidence in the Brooks Range suggests that at this subduction zone, which is informally known as the Kobuk suture zone, more than 400 miles of continental crust has been overridden and scraped up as major thrust sheets to form the mountains.

However, about 130 million years ago, during the collision, the process was complicated by a rifting event to the north, in which northern Alaska assumed its final form. Many geologists believe that northern Alaska, including the developing Brooks Range, rotated counterclockwise away from northern Canada to form the Canada Basin of the Arctic Ocean north of Alaska. This event resulted in the presence of a deep ocean basin in an area that we know from the sedimentary record to have earlier been for a long period of time an uplifted source of sediments. It is this process of subduction, which telescoped, stacked and folded the various distinctive strata of northern Alaska, followed by rifting, that gives the Brooks Range its unique character that differs so from the other ranges in Alaska.

As the process of uplift in the Brooks Range and rifting along the arctic coast progressed, vast amounts of sediment were eroded off the mountains and poured into a deep sedimentary basin that formed north of the mountains. This basin, known as the Colville Basin, underlies most of the North Slope and has progressively filled with sediment — a process that continues today.

The Brooks Range begins as a geologic and

A small tarn awaits hikers crossing 4,050-foot Angunelechek Pass through the Schwatka Mountains southwest of Mount Igikpak (8,510 feet). (Jon R. Nickles)

topographic entity at the Blow River, about 80 miles east of the international boundary, in Canada's Yukon Territory. It first forms a range of low hills known as the Barn Mountains, which, at the Blow River, are less than 25 miles in width. The highest point in the Barn Mountains is barely over 4,000 feet, and average summits are around 3,500 feet elevation. The Blow River separates the Barn Mountains from the geologically and topographically distinct north-south trending Richardson Mountains, which are the main physiographic feature in the northern part of Yukon Territory.

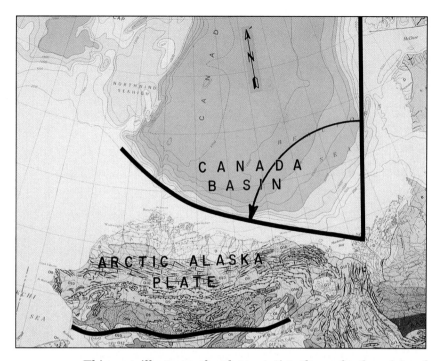

This map illustrates the plate rotation theory for the origin of northern Alaska. A number of earth scientists believe that the Brooks Range was formed when a piece of the continent rotated counter-clockwise away from the Arctic Islands in Canada. The theory suggests that the mountains were formed by the snowplowlike effect of the continental crust colliding with another piece of the crust to the south. Simultaneously with the rotation, the southern Arctic Ocean basin north of Alaska was formed. (Gil Mull)

West of the Barn Mountains, the British Mountains and Buckland Hills trend northwest toward the Alaska boundary, rising steadily in height and width. In the area of 141 degrees west longitude, the Alaska-Yukon boundary, the Brooks Range has grown to more than 80 miles in width, with peaks over 5,000 feet separated by a rugged terrain of steep-walled canyons, a sharp contrast to the broad rolling valleys in the Barn Mountains.

Just west of the Alaska-Yukon boundary, the British Mountains swing to a more nearly east-west trend and merge into the Romanzof Mountains in the heart of the Arctic National Wildlife Refuge. To many people, the eastern part of the refuge contains the most scenic and most fascinating portion of the entire 720-mile length of the Brooks Range.

In the wildlife refuge, the mountains reach both their highest and widest points, more than 110 miles from north to south. Near the international boundary, there are miles of jumbled, jagged peaks underlain by early Paleozoic and Precambrian sedimentary, metamorphic and volcanic rocks.

Light-gray-weathering Lisburne limestone forms spectacular cliffs in some areas. Farther west, the high peaks of the Romanzof and neighboring Franklin Mountains, indeed, the highest peaks in the entire Brooks Range — Mount Isto, 9,060 feet; Mount Chamberlin, 9,020 feet; Mount Hubley, 8,915 feet — are glacier-mantled and to some people are the scenic climax of the Arctic refuge.

Chamberlin is formed of somber metasediments, metamorphosed sedimentary rocks whose sediments have been partially transformed but never totally melted, while Hubley and adjacent peaks are carved from light-colored granite. These rise abruptly from the 2,000-foot northern foothills. The approximately 7,000 feet of vertical relief makes these quite respectable mountains in anybody's book, even though their absolute height is not as great as many peaks in other Alaska ranges.

Other special points of interest in the eastern refuge include Ignek Valley, which separates the Sadlerochit and Shublik

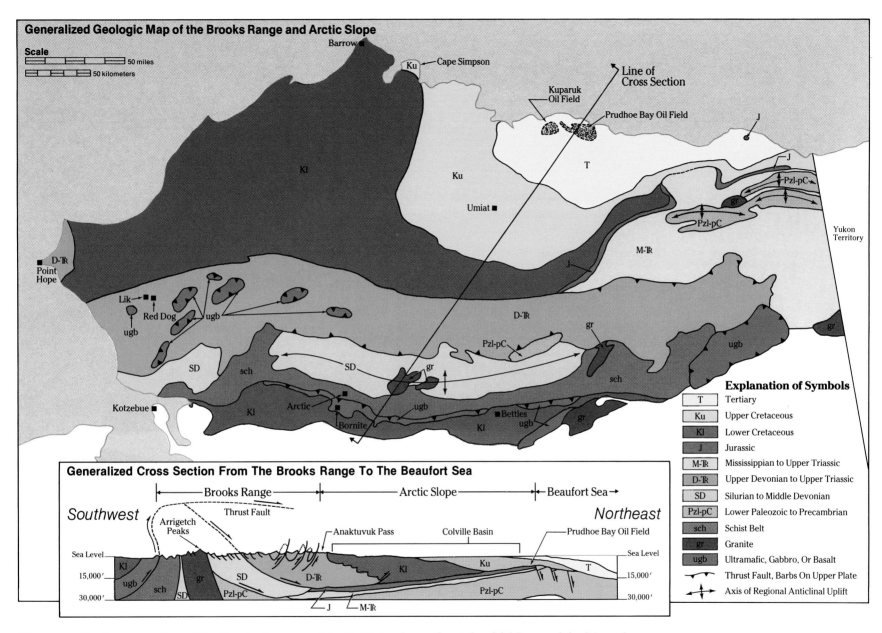

Generalized Geologic Map of the Brooks Range and Arctic Slope

Scale
50 miles
50 kilometers

Barrow
Cape Simpson
Ku
Line of Cross Section
Kuparuk Oil Field
Prudhoe Bay Oil Field
Ku
Kl
T
Umiat
M-TR
J
J
Pzl-pC
Pzl-pC
gr
Yukon Territory
D-TR
Point Hope
Lik
Red Dog
ugb
ugb
SD
sch
SD
D-TR
gr
Pzl-pC
gr
ugb
sch
Kotzebue
Kl
Arctic
ugb
Bettles
gr
Bornite
Kl
ugb

Explanation of Symbols

T	Tertiary
Ku	Upper Cretaceous
Kl	Lower Cretaceous
J	Jurassic
M-TR	Mississippian to Upper Triassic
D-TR	Upper Devonian to Upper Triassic
SD	Silurian to Middle Devonian
Pzl-pC	Lower Paleozoic to Precambrian
sch	Schist Belt
gr	Granite
ugb	Ultramafic, Gabbro, Or Basalt
⌄⌄	Thrust Fault, Barbs On Upper Plate
↔	Axis of Regional Anticlinal Uplift

Generalized Cross Section From The Brooks Range To The Beaufort Sea

|← Brooks Range →|← Arctic Slope →|← Beaufort Sea →|

Southwest

Thrust Fault
Arrigetch Peaks
Anaktuvuk Pass
Colville Basin
Prudhoe Bay Oil Field
Northeast
Sea Level
Kl
ugb
sch
gr
SD
SD
Pzl-pC
D-TR
Kl
Ku
T
Sea Level
15,000'
15,000'
30,000'
Pzl-pC
30,000'
J
M-TR

The generalized cross section of the Brooks Range and Arctic Slope shows the style of folding and faulting of the major rock units of northern Alaska. In the generalized geologic map of the Brooks Range and Arctic Slope, the colors show approximate areas of exposure of distinctive rocks of various ages in northern Alaska. (Graphic by Jon. Hersh, reprinted from ALASKA GEOGRAPHIC®, Vol. 9, No. 4, 1982)

mountains, and lakes Schrader and Peters, located at the foot of Mount Chamberlin. Ignek Valley is a tundra-mantled east-west trending valley with scattered bright-red-weathering patches of Cretaceous sediment, flanked on both sides by contrasting white limestone cliffs.

Ikiakpuk Valley, an isolated valley on the east side of the Canning River near the mountain front, contains a large grove of trees, mostly balsam poplar and hybrid birch. This grove, on the supposedly treeless North Slope, probably represents the northernmost trees in Alaska, and perhaps in North America. At least three other groves, all composed of representatives of the birch and cottonwood families, are found in sheltered valleys on the slope.

West of the Canning River lie the Philip Smith Mountains, named for the onetime head

of the U.S. Geological Survey's Alaska section. These mountains, which form the western part of the Arctic National Wildlife Refuge, are characterized mostly by precipitous valleys cut into miles of intricately folded and faulted light gray cliffs of Lisburne limestone.

But, deep within the mountains, a secluded unnamed valley that extends from the Ivishak River eastward to the upper Canning River contrasts sharply with the jagged Lisburne limestone cliffs. South of the Continental

BELOW: *Calls of the common loon leave haunting images in the memories of Brooks Range travelers. Their early morning and late evening calls and their pattering across a lake's surface add comedy and theatrics to a northern sojourn. (Chlaus Lotscher)*

RIGHT: *Among the most popular routes for river running in the Arctic National Wildlife Refuge is the Kongakut, which flows 100 miles from the Davidson Mountains to the Beaufort Sea in extreme northeastern Alaska. (Chlaus Lotscher)*

Hiking at lower elevations in the Brooks Range can be tough going, but once above treeline, hikers find the ridges and open tundra much friendlier to their feet and clothing. Here Jon Nickles prepares a meal on a ridge above the Dietrich River valley. (Jon R. Nickles)

glacial epoch, and are characterized by broad U-shaped, glacially carved valleys. However, only a few small isolated cirque glaciers now remain in sheltered areas on some of the higher peaks.

Westward, the Philip Smith Mountains merge almost imperceptibly into the Endicott Mountains near Atigun Pass, through which the Dalton Highway and trans-Alaska pipeline cross the Brooks Range. The Dalton Highway, which was built by the oil industry to support the development of the Prudhoe Bay oil field on the shore of the Beaufort Sea 150 miles north of the range front, provides the only road access to the Brooks Range. The highway can be reached from the Elliott Highway north of Fairbanks, about 350 miles south of the Brooks Range crest at Atigun Pass. This highway corridor separates the Arctic refuge on the east from Gates of the Arctic National Park to the west. Coldfoot, where the road enters the southern flank of the range, offers food, lodging and limited road services, and is the site of a visitors center maintained by the National Park Service, Bureau of Land Management and Fish and Wildlife Service, which administer most of the public lands in the Brooks Range. Wiseman, a historical mining camp just west of the Dalton Highway north of Coldfoot, was the center for pioneering conservationist Robert Marshall's explorations in the 1930s. Other scenic highlights along the Dalton Highway include Mount Sukakpak in the Dietrich River valley north of Wiseman, and Atigun Gorge, just east of the highway near the northern mountain front. The gorge, which offers easy hiking, is flanked on the south by high Lisburne limestone cliffs, over which a scenic waterfall

Divide in the refuge, several major tributary valleys cut through miles of Lisburne limestone and lead southward to the East Fork of the Chandalar River and Arctic Village — home of the Gwich'in, Athabaskan Indians who occupy the only permanent settlement of any size in the eastern Brooks Range.

The Philip Smith Mountains were extensively glaciated during the Pleistocene

plunges about three miles east of the road. The north side of the gorge is formed by sandstone and conglomerate of the Fortress Mountain formation, composed of debris eroded during Cretaceous time from the rising Brooks Range.

West of the Dalton Highway, Gates of the Arctic National Park encompasses most of the Endicott Mountains, which have peaks ranging from 6,500 to about 8,000 feet. Pleistocene glaciers also left major signs of their presence in the Endicott Mountains, but the remaining modern glaciers are generally small and confined to cirques and valleys on the north side of the higher peaks. The Endicott Mountains maintain a fairly uniform character for more than 200 miles westward past Anaktuvuk Pass, a major low-level access route through the mountains and the site of the only settlement within the main part of the Brooks Range. Anaktuvuk Pass is inhabited by a group of formerly nomadic Inupiat Eskimo known as the Nunamiut. The settlement is located at the base of spectacular light gray cliffs of the Lisburne limestone, which forms much of the northern flank of the range, and is certainly the most scenic settlement in northern Alaska. With a good all-weather airstrip, Anaktuvuk is an increasingly popular destination for hikers who either begin or end cross-country tours of parts of Gates of the Arctic National Park there. Graylime Creek and Cocked Hat Mountain are

The Arrigetch Peaks area ranks as one of the top attractions for visitors to the Brooks Range. The 6,000 to 7,200-foot granite spires are usually reached from the Alatna River valley. (Jon R. Nickles)

The John River flows south out of the Brooks Range through the heart of Alaska's taiga, the circumpolar boreal forest. The river runs 125 miles from Anaktuvuk Pass to the Koyukuk River one mile from Bettles. (Chlaus Lotscher)

among the most spectacular areas in this part of the national park, and the traverse up the Anaktuvuk River and through Ernie Pass to the North Fork of the Koyukuk and Mount Doonerak (7,610 feet) is a popular route.

The crest of the central Brooks Range is formed by somber brown conglomerate and sandstone of the Devonian Kanayut conglomerate, deposited about 360 million years ago. South of the divide, Mount Doonerak and the North Fork of the Koyukuk River are popular destinations for hiking and river-rafting.

In the western Endicott Mountains, west of Kurupa Lake, the extensive Lisburne limestone terrain that forms the mountain front of most of the central and eastern Brooks Range is replaced by reddish-brown-to-black-weathering peaks of Kanayut sandstone. The average elevation decreases rapidly through Howard Pass and on to Feniak Lake, where the Endicott Mountains disappear as a geologic and topographic entity.

To the south, the Schwatka Mountains have maximum elevations of between 8,000 and

ABOVE RIGHT: *An estimated 30,000 Dall sheep roam the Brooks Range, about one-third of them grazing on upper slopes of north-flowing rivers in the Arctic refuge. To survive the severe winters of the Arctic, the sheep forage on ridges and north-facing slopes that receive less snowfall and where winds can blow the snow away, exposing the vegetation on which the sheep feed. (Chlaus Lotscher)*

RIGHT: *A cow moose and her calf forage along the Killik River on the north flank of the Brooks Range. (Chlaus Lotscher)*

LEFT: *The Alatna River serves as a major route for travel in the central Brooks Range. Here Awlinyak Creek flows 18 miles northeast to join the Alatna south of Survey Pass. (Jon R. Nickles)*

ABOVE: *A handful of Alaskans live year-round in the tiny community of Wiseman, a former mining boomtown on the banks of the Middle Fork of the Koyukuk River. In the first decades of the 20th century, Wiseman, neighboring Coldfoot and other communities, now abandoned, were part of a gold rush to upper Koyukuk country. (Patrick J. Endres)*

FACING PAGE: *Gaby Husmann explores steep slopes of the Franklin Mountains above the Hulahula River in the Arctic National Wildlife Refuge. (Chlaus Lotscher)*

8,800 feet, and decrease rapidly to the west. These mountains contain another truly spectacular segment of the Brooks Range — the Arrigetch Peaks and Mount Igikpak. Both areas are formed in granites, something of a rarity elsewhere in the Brooks Range, and have been scoured into Yosemitelike valleys by glaciers,

One of the few year-round residents of Brooks Range country who chose to live away from any established community was Ed Owens. In the 1950s, Owens and his wife lived on the Coleen River, where they raised a family. Each year Owens would build a boat that he rowed to Fort Yukon, where he sold it, bought supplies and flew back to the Coleen River. This photo shows Owens and one of his boats in 1962. (G.H. Pessel, courtesy of Gil Mull)

remnants of which remain. The Arrigetch Peaks and Mount Igikpak have been described as "probably the finest mountains in Arctic Alaska" by David Roberts. The area has become popular with technical mountain climbers, who are attracted by the challenge of the sheer, vertical granite walls and the lure of highly technical ascents, some of which have entered mountaineering annals. The first ascents of many of the Arrigetch Peaks were not made until 1964. Others were made in 1969 by a party that included Roberts. Mount Igikpak (8,510 feet), the highest peak in the central Brooks Range, was first climbed in 1968; its summit was described by Roberts, who made the first ascent, as a 200-foot cylinder with a mushroomlike block overhanging on all sides, that was "easily the most remarkable summit any of us had ever been on, a little platform, it seemed, in extraterrestrial space...." The Alatna River and upper Noatak River that bound the Arrigetch Peaks and Mount Igikpak are accessible by floatplane and are access routes for climbers in the area. West of Mount Igikpak, the western Schwatka Mountains, which merge westward with the Baird Mountains, are characterized by a terrain of widespread early Paleozoic limestone, 50 million years older than the Lisburne of the DeLong Mountains to the north.

In the far western Brooks Range, the DeLong and Baird mountains are separated by the valley of the Noatak River, which flows westward through Noatak National Preserve from its headwaters in Gates of the Arctic National Park in the Schwatka Mountains. The DeLong and Baird mountains are much lower and more subdued in general character than are the mountains to the east. Elevations are all less than 5,000 feet, most less than 4,000 feet. Although isolated areas of spectacular scenery occur in this portion of the range, it generally lacks the scenic allure of the central and eastern Brooks Range. Somewhat like the Barn Mountains at the easternmost end of the Brooks Range, the peaks in this waning phase of the mountain mass are mostly separated by broad alluvial valleys.

And, finally, at the western end, where the geologic Brooks Range runs out to sea, the mountains are characterized by barren, light gray, rubble-covered rolling hills, tapering below less than 2,000 feet in elevation. Although the coastal Lisburne Hills are held up by the same Lisburne limestone unit that forms some of the highest and most rugged portions of the Endicott and Philip Smith mountains, here on the west, the range is only a shadow of its former self.

The entire Brooks Range is the main divide between drainage northward into the Arctic Ocean, and drainage west and south into the Yukon, Kobuk and Noatak rivers. Although the range crest is an effective divide in most places, some individual river systems completely transect the range and rise on the side opposite that to which they eventually flow. For example, the Firth and Kongakut rivers rise on the south, cut through the main spine of the range and flow into the Arctic Ocean near the Alaska-Yukon boundary. The John River, at Anaktuvuk Pass, does the reverse, rising on the north and flowing south to transect the mountains. This reversal in drainages probably results in part from the extreme effect of glaciation during the Pleistocene glacial ages.

Fall comes to Tulilik Lake near the junction of the Killik River and Easter Creek in Gates of the Arctic Wilderness Area. (Chlaus Lotscher)

From Anaktuvuk Pass westward there are a number of broad glacially alluviated valleys such as the Killik and upper Alatna that offer essentially water-level routes across the mountains. The Nigu and Etivluk rivers, which are tributaries of the Colville River on the North Slope, provide access routes into the Noatak River drainage through low passes such as Howard Pass.

One of the attractions of the central and eastern Brooks Range are the large, glacial-moraine-dammed lakes, which are found at

One of the highest peak in the Brooks Range, Mount Chamberlin, 9,020 feet, rises in the Franklin Mountains of the Arctic National Wildlife Refuge. Just to the east of the Franklin Mountains across the valley of the Hulahula River lie the Romanzof Mountains, topped by Mount Hubley, 8,915 feet, and Mount Isto, 9,060 feet. This trio represent the highest peaks in the Brooks Range and from these slopes flow some of the few glaciers found within the range. (Chlaus Lotscher)

intervals on both the north and south sides. Schrader, Peters, Elusive, Shainin, Chandler, Kurupa, Walker, Wild and Chandalar lakes, to name some, provide easy access by floatplane to many of the remote areas of the mountains. Numerous other small and not so small lakes are found in many of the major river valleys.

The Brooks Range is also the major climatic divide that separates the Interior from the Arctic. Spruce trees, for example, are confined to the warmer southern valleys of the range, except for a stand near the middle part of the Firth River, east of the Yukon boundary.

Throughout its length, the Brooks Range is a study in contrast, with some areas of spectacular beauty and other large portions that are rather drab by comparison. In some areas at some times of the year, wildlife is abundant. Caribou, in particular, are abundant in June and July on the coastal plain north of the mountains. The annual migration of the Porcupine caribou herd in the Arctic refuge is spectacular to behold for those fortunate enough to be at the right place at the right time. Similarly, the migration of the western Arctic caribou herd through the range is a spectacular event that is occasionally observed by the lucky visitor.

Barren ground grizzlies are found throughout the Brooks Range, and Dall sheep are common in some of the higher areas of the central and eastern Brooks Range. But, in some areas the visitor may spend weeks without seeing a trace of major wild game.

In June and July some hillsides may be alive with the color of tiny tundra flowers, but many weathered, rock-covered slopes are bare and devoid of plant life. Summertime days can be idyllic, with temperatures in the 70s and 24 hours of sunshine. But, such days can be

BELOW LEFT: *A roughlegged hawk glares at intruders from its rocky perch above the Canning River. (George Wuerthner)*

BELOW: *Dan Stack flips a pancake under the watchful gaze of Allison Butler while on a hiking excursion through the westcentral Brooks Range. Natural fuel is difficult to find in many areas of the range and what trees and shrubs do occur grow slowly because of the northern climate. Visitors should bring camp stoves and plenty of fuel. (Jon R. Nickles)*

followed by blizzards that give the land the appearance of midwinter and drop temperatures into the teens. On warm, calm days from late June to early August, while the tundra is green and breeding spots abound, hordes of mosquitoes can at times make life nearly intolerable, even on high rocky slopes and peaks hundreds of feet above the nearest potential mosquito-breeding grounds. These insects can drive caribou and man, without adequate repellent or protection, nearly wild in attempts to escape the constant buzzing and biting. By mid-August, however, the ever-shortening days and decreasing temperatures mercifully eliminate the mosquitoes, and herald the end of summer. The early fall storms begin to drop the snow level ever lower on the mountain peaks and, in contrast to the midsummer storms, these snows will not melt before the following spring. The intense sub-zero cold of midwinter can be a time of silent beauty. But, it also can be a time of howling winds that drive dense clouds of drifting snow through the mountain valleys. The Brooks Range can be a land that offers great enjoyment in exploration, but it is not a land for the unprepared or the careless — even in midsummer.

The Inupiat on the north and west and Athabaskans on the south, of course, knew all about the Brooks Range long before the first white man came to record observations on

A hiker roams the Kongakut River valley, which receives some of the highest visitor use within the 19-plus-million-acre Arctic National Wildlife Refuge. (Chlaus Lotscher)

Everything from crackers to rifles to T-shirts is available at the Wiseman Trading Post. Wiseman lies a short way off the Dalton Highway on the south side of the Brooks Range and supplies can now come in by vehicle. In earlier times, most residents of the upper Koyukuk region got their supplies by river. From Bettles, shallow scows carried freight upriver to the mining communities. (Patrick J. Endres)

paper. Much of the early recorded exploration of the range by white men was by scientific expeditions, which included both private and government-funded efforts. Although gold rush prospectors penetrated into the southern margin of the range in the late 19th century, most of these pioneer explorers in search of mineral wealth left little permanent record of their passing.

The early prospectors were successful in discovering gold in the Chandalar and

LEFT: *The trans-Alaska pipeline and Dalton Highway pass by this lake in the Saganvanirktok Valley. The valley is the main corridor from the mountains to Deadhorse and the oil complex at Prudhoe Bay. (Pete Martin)*

BELOW: *These zinc and copper sulfides, targets of mineral exploration, were unearthed in the central Brooks Range. (Bill Sherwonit)*

Caribou cross in front of a plane tied to barrels anchored in the ice of Takahula Lake. The plane is on wheels in winter; nearby sit the floats that will be attached for summer travel. (Tom Falley)

Wiseman areas, and production from small placer mines near Wiseman, where a 42-ounce nugget was found in 1995, continues to this day. Later exploration for base metals resulted in discovery of significant reserves at Bornite and Arctic Camp, in the southern Brooks Range near Kobuk and Shungnak, and in the world class zinc-lead deposit at Red Dog, now in production in the western DeLong Mountains north of Kotzebue.

Much of the early recorded exploration of

BELOW: *A cushion or dwarf hawk's-beard blossoms near the headwaters of the Nigu River in the westcentral Brooks Range. The Nigu begins in Imakturok Pass and flows northwest 70 miles to the Etivluk River. Nigu is an Inupiaq description for rainbow, and a name applied to a chert bluff past which the river flows. (Nancy Falley)*

RIGHT: *The trans-Alaska oil pipeline runs 800 miles from Prudhoe Bay on the Arctic Ocean to the ice-free port of Valdez on Prince William Sound. Construction began on the pipeline in 1974 and concluded in 1977. Nine operating pump stations control movement of the oil through the 48-inch-diameter pipe, about half of which is aboveground. The pipeline rests on vertical support members; heat fins on the supports let off heat generated by activity within the pipeline. The oil moves at approximately 6 1/2 mph and requires five and one-half days to go from Pump Station 1 to the marine terminal at Valdez. (Patrick J. Endres)*

the northern Brooks Range was carried out by geologists of the U.S. Geological Survey, who mapped both the rocks and the topography and recorded both the Native names and attached numerous new names to the rivers and mountains. This geological exploration occurred in several waves, beginning with F.C. Schrader in the central Brooks Range in 1899,

John Dillon (1947-1987), left, and Irv Tailleur collect rock samples on a ridge above the Okpilak River. Dillon Mountain (4,820 feet), northeast of Mount Sukakpak, is named for Dillon, a long-time geologist with the Alaska Division of Geological and Geophysical Surveys who did extensive mapping of mineral occurrences in the southern Brooks Range. (Arne Bakke)

and Ernest de Koven Leffingwell in a privately funded expedition to the northeastern Brooks Range from 1907 to 1914. A second wave of exploration occurred in the mid-1920s when Naval Petroleum Reserve #4 was established on the north side of the mountains. These were major lengthy expeditions by dog team, boat and foot. A third wave by the USGS and the Navy in search of petroleum resources in NPR-4 began in the 1940s, aided by aircraft. Yet a fourth wave of exploration for petroleum on the North Slope began in the late 1950s, this time by private industry and with the continuing participation of government. Although the mountain areas were known to have no petroleum potential, these geologists, supported by reliable helicopters, penetrated into the remotest areas of the range in search of technical data that might yield clues to areas of interest beneath the foothills and coastal plain north of the mountains.

In 1968, the scientific efforts were successful, with the discovery of the Prudhoe Bay oil field — the largest petroleum accumulation in North America — which resulted in construction of the Dalton Highway and the trans-Alaska pipeline. This highway, for better or worse, has opened a small part of the central Brooks Range to easy access by ordinary passenger cars and campers, and has had a noticeable impact on the wilderness character of the narrow corridor through which it passes. But, this single corridor is the only significant mark of man visible to a pilot, who could fly the entire 600-mile length of the range in Alaska without observing another sign of man's impact on this, the state's most remote mountain range. ■

Tumultuous geology in ancient times has resulted in the spectacular bedding found in the rocks of the upper west fork of the Itkillik River valley. (Gil Mull)

A Tenderfoot Tiptoes Into the Brooks Range

By Penny Rennick

The first time I saw the Brooks Range, I was sitting amidst a field of fireweed at Bettles, waiting for a bush plane to fly me to Takahula Lake. I remember squinting through my binoculars, trying to figure out just what peaks were Bob Marshall's "Gates of the Arctic." This was 20 years ago, before a national park adopted Marshall's slogan, when my knowlege of the Brooks Range was made up of nine parts myth and one part fact.

Our tiny band had been headed to Walker Lake for a two-week camping adventure, but reports of overly rambunctious bears at the lake prompted our guide to detour to Takahula. The pilot had to fly two trips to get us and our gear to the north shore of the lake where we would sleep two to a tent. We cooked out of doors: freeze-dried stew, stroganoff, chicken and biscuits, supplemented with local mushrooms, cranberries and blueberries that had ripened in the late August sun.

Bears were on everyone's mind, especially after the reports from Walker Lake. Every night

I lay awake as long as possible, just in case. My tentmate was a graduate student from back East who had been employed as naturalist for the summer. One night early in our stay, I was convinced a bear was just outside the tent. I strained to hear every footstep. Afraid to move, yet equally afraid not to, I looked at my tentmate. She was sound asleep.

Finally, I dug around in my gear, as quietly as possible, and pulled out my Swiss Army knife. The movement awakened my tentmate,

LEFT: *Summer visitors to the Brooks Range may see the American golden plover, a classy shorebird that prefers drier tundra for its summer breeding and foraging. (Chlaus Lotscher)*

FACING PAGE: *A fringe of aspen decorates the forested skirt of this Brooks Range peak overlooking the middle fork of the Dietrich River near Dietrich Camp. (Patrick J. Endres)*

who naturally wondered why I was sitting on top of my sleeping bag in my flannel pajamas with a pocket knife in my hand, its longest blade pointed toward the tent's front flap.

"There's a bear out there." She gave me an incredulous look. But I was certain. There were sounds, and they seemed to be circling the tent. She remained dubious, but after a half hour or so, my fear got the better of her common sense and she became convinced that there was indeed an animal out there. She got out of her bag and we both sat in the middle of the tent, me with a knife, she with a flashlight. It was getting cold, and we kept wondering why the animal didn't attack or go away. It just kept circling the tent.

Finally my tentmate could stand the tension no longer. She put on her shoes and coat, grabbed the flashlight, and stuck her head

ABOVE LEFT: *A camper's tent brightens a bog in the Junjik River valley in the southeastern Brooks Range. The Junjik flows 65 miles from the mountains to enter the East Fork Chandalar River a few miles northwest of the Gwich'in Athabaskan community of Arctic Village. (George Wuerthner)*

ABOVE: *Red Morton of Chickaloon, Alaska, packs up after a successful Dall sheep hunt near Roche Moutonnee Creek. (Patrick J. Endres)*

Caribou and northern Alaska seem to go hand in hand. At least three distinct herds roam the region: the Western Arctic, the Central Arctic and the Porcupine. Each spring and fall these herds migrate through the Brooks Range to calving or wintering grounds. (Tom Falley)

out the flap. She saw nothing, and the sound had stopped. I stuck my head out, same result. We both got up and circled the tent. No other animals were in evidence.

We returned to our sleeping bags, and all I can say is that I deserve an A for powers of persuasion and an F for knowledge of animal sounds. My bear was the rain falling on the tent. And a few nights later, when a moose did circle the tent, I slept through the entire event.

My first experience in the Brooks Range is typical of that of many recreationists. Opportunities for river rafting and backpacking/camping in the wilderness lure most visitors to this northern rampart. People expect to BE in the wilderness when they hit the Brooks Range. Sometimes though this wilderness can get a little crowded.

Our group looked forward to two weeks hiking in the Takahula area, picking blueberries and cranberries in the bog at the south end of the lake, watching the gray jays gliding near our campsite and the mink family that patrolled the lake's eastern shore. In the evening before dinner, we would listen for the arctic loons chortling to one another, and for the high-pitched squeak of a vole family that came and went from a tundra-and-shrub maze surrounding one of the spruce at the campsite. So sure were we that this was our little corner of

the Brooks Range that we were actually upset one evening when, as we listened for the loons, we heard distinctly unloonlike sounds coming from the trees flanking a low ridge separating Takahula from the Alatna River. A scan to the east with our binoculars rewarded us with a view of binoculars looking back. We had company. A rafting party had, like the bear, decided to go over the mountain to see what was there. What they found was us. Fortunately they were no more excited to see us than we were to see them, so they quickly departed.

Jeff Mow, a ranger with Gates of the Arctic National Park, says river rafting brings the most recreationists to the central Brooks Range. Visitors can drive the Dalton Highway, leave their vehicle at one of several parking areas or at Nolan, which has designated parking, and hike into the park from the east. More often, however, visitors charter a bush flight into one of the lakes or rivers and begin their journey by water. Both the Noatak and Kobuk rivers, the major drainages of northwestern Alaska, begin in Gates of the Arctic. The Noatak is the most popular river for rafting in the western part of the park, says Mow, because it is the easiest to float, the country is more open, the river has few dangerous spots and opportunities to see wildlife abound. Air taxis generally use three put-in spots to discharge rafters heading down the Noatak: These locations go by the

Road dust trails behind a truck traveling the Dalton Highway near the pipeline. The road is 28 feet wide and covered with 3 to 6 feet of gravel, and motorists should be alert for dust, flying gravel and reduced visibility when trucks pass by. (Patrick J. Endres)

A kayaker lines her kayak along a braided channel of the Canning River, which forms part of the western boundary of the Arctic National Wildlife Refuge. (George Wuerthner)

local names of 12-Mile Slough, Pingo Lake and Nelson Walker Lake. The latter is named for a hunting guide who had a series of cabins on the upper Noatak.

The Kobuk River sees much less rafting traffic but those who do come this way usually put in at Walker Lake, a large lake near the park's southern boundary. One reason the Kobuk has less rafting is the presence of two canyons, Upper and Lower Kobuk, that require portages of 1/2 to 3/4 miles. People have run the canyons, says Mow, but people have also been killed doing so. Upper Kobuk country is generally steeper than that of the upper Noatak, although the forest is open and the footing good as long as travelers can circumvent the dangers of the river. From Walker Lake some hikers head cross-country to the Noatak drainage.

Next to floating the two rivers, the Arrigetch Peaks area receives the greatest visitor load in the western Gates of the Arctic. Pilots generally drop off hikers at an old river channel known locally as Circle Lake, about 2 miles south of where Arrigetch Creek enters the Alatna.

There is little winter recreational activity in the western park because access is difficult. As Mow says, it is "a long way from nowhere." Trappers and subsistence hunters use the park in winter and there is some travel by year-round residents between the Inupiat villages of Anaktuvuk Pass and Ambler on the Kobuk River. Hunting and trapping in the park is allowed for residents under provisions for local rural subsistence.

Winter recreational activities pick up somewhat in the eastern Gates of the Arctic because the Dalton Highway, open year-round

RIGHT: *The federal Bureau of Land Management, National Park Service and U.S. Fish and Wildlife Service jointly operate this visitor center at Coldfoot at milepost 175 of the Dalton Highway. (Tom Culkin)*

BELOW RIGHT: *Long-abandoned Native dwellings near Cape Lisburne lie in the shadow of the Lisburne Hills, the western extremity of the Brooks Range. (Gil Mull)*

to travelers, increases access. At its closest point, the eastern boundary of the park is two miles from the highway. There are winter dogsled trips into the park from Bettles and Coldfoot.

One of the more popular summer destinations says Glen Dodson, East District Ranger for the park, are the two mountains that Bob Marshall immortalized. Boreal Mountain and Frigid Crags make up the "Gates" and can be reached after a strenuous hike from the Dalton Highway. "Gates"-seekers have to traverse the range adjacent to the highway on the west and then work their way through another range before they can reach the two mountains. There are no established trails to the "Gates;" in fact, the National Park Service has established no trails within the entire 8.5-million-acre park and preserve. This is wilderness and fixed trails are discouraged. So reaching the "Gates," as with all areas of the Brooks Range, requires having wilderness travel savvy, bringing proper equipment and supplies, studying a good map and picking a route that leads reasonably from one drainage to another.

Near the "Gates" there are put-in spots

Snow and ice collect in the south valley of the Arrigetch Peaks in the heart of the Brooks Range. The mountain chain is named for Alfred Hulse Brooks, an 1894 geology graduate of Harvard, who first came to Alaska in 1898 as a geologist for the U.S. Geological Survey. For 23 years Brooks headed Alaska geology work for the government. Born in 1871, Brooks collapsed and died at his desk in Washington D.C. in 1924. Mount Brooks in Denali National Park and Brooks lake and falls in Katmai National Park are also named for him. (Tom Falley)

LEFT: *Dan Stack fords the Noatak River, followed by Allison Butler and Mike Wiedmer. (Jon R. Nickles)*

BELOW LEFT: *The windflower or northern anemone occurs throughout much of Alaska in arctic and alpine tundra, and in lower elevation woodlands and heathlands. (Pete Martin)*

BELOW: *For some, northern Alaska conjures up images of a year-round refrigerator, perpetual ice and snow. In reality, the short, frenetic summer that characterizes the high Arctic teems with life, including tundra-covered slopes sparkling with wildflowers. In addition to their beauty, arctic plants have proved useful to residents and visitors to the region for their medicinal or food values. For instance, Natives of the upper Koyukuk use Labrador tea and rose hips to ward off scurvy, a disease caused by a deficiency of vitamin C. (Patrick J. Endres)*

LEFT: *Caribou pass through the Alatna River valley during fall migration. (Chlaus Lotscher)*

BELOW LEFT: *The only services between the Yukon River and Deadhorse are at Coldfoot at mile 175 of the Dalton Highway. (Chlaus Lotscher)*

along the North Fork of the Koyukuk River, and at Summit Lake and Red Star Lake. Air taxis can land on the lakes or on gravel bars along the river. It's about 120 river miles from the "Gates," to Bettles, at the junction of the John and Koyukuk rivers and gateway to much of the central Brooks Range.

On the north side of the Brooks Range, rafters head for the Nigu, Itkillik, Killik and Anaktuvuk rivers. Although none of these rivers receive much traffic, the Killik draws the greatest share of these adventurous travelers.

Toward the end of our stay at Takahula, our contingent decided that it too should sample a Brooks Range river, so we drug our aluminum canoe over the low ridge and through the forest to the sandy banks of the Alatna. We launched on a sunny midmorning in early September, paddling down a wide meander of the river. About 12 miles downstream, our leader decided to turn up a stream entering the Alatna from the west. This was supposed to lead us back to the southern shore of Takahula Lake. But our leader forgot the warning printed in many backcountry brochures. Late in the summer, Brooks Range rivers tend to run out of enough water for travel. After paddling upstream for some distance, our creek gave out and we had to drag the canoe out of the channel. It was a long hike to get back to our camp by dusk. Two

days later when the air taxi flew us back to Bettles, my parting image of Takahula was of a canoe sitting high and dry in a field crowded with blueberries.

• • •

Noatak National Preserve flanks Gates of the Arctic on the west; the Arctic National Wildlife Refuge does the same on the east. Here, too, rivers are a prime attraction. The most popular runs in the refuge flow northward to the Arctic Ocean: the Hulahula, Kongakut, Canning. Air taxis from Fort Yukon drop passengers off at gravel and dirt strips deep in the mountains. Southward-bound travelers usually choose the Sheenjek River, which flows 240 miles through a boreal wilderness to dump into the Porcupine River 40 miles out from Fort Yukon.

It was this lure of the rivers that once again drew me north. Fifteen years after I'd tiptoed through the Alatna Valley I was back in the Brooks Range, ready to float the Hulahula. By this time I'd had a whole lot more experience with the Alaska Bush and I looked forward to 10 days coasting and bumping downriver to the arctic shore. But the Brooks Range and its rivers weren't through with me yet. This time the problem wasn't the lack of water, it was too much water.

This year by the end of June the Hulahula was carrying more than its share of Brooks Range runoff. The late Joe Firmin, pilot for our

Late winter snow and a returning sun highlight this view of 14-mile-long Walker Lake, among the largest lakes within Gates of the Arctic National Park. (Tom Falley)

bush flight, landed at a gravel strip known as Grassers near the river's headwaters early in the afternoon. We had the rest of the day, and night since darkness does not come to the range at this time of year, to explore a nearby collapsed pingo and hike whatever valleys intrigued us. I flushed an American tree sparrow from her nest and spent the rest of the time inspecting the shrubs for other nests.

Early the next morning we launched our attack on the Hulahula. Even though the water level was high, the braided channel and our fully loaded raft meant we frequently bottomed out. We would pile into the raft, paddle left or right on directions from our guide who was perched in the stern with one or two hands on the tiller, and slowly work our way downstream

ABOVE LEFT: *High, rocky sea cliffs tower over the Chukchi coast from Cape Lisburne (shown here) south to Cape Thompson. This coast is home to numerous seabirds, including thick-billed and common murres, black-legged kittiwakes and horned puffins, and parts of it lie within the Chukchi Sea unit of the Alaska Maritime National Wildlife Refuge. About 50 million seabirds breed along Alaska's coast, more than in the rest of North America. (Gil Mull)*

LEFT: *A Super Cub uses the Dalton Highway north of Atigun Pass as a landing strip. The highway is named for arctic engineer James W. Dalton, who participated in early exploration for oil on the North Slope. Construction of the road began April 29, 1974, and was completed five months later. It was originally called the North Slope Haul Road and was built to aid construction of the trans-Alaska pipeline. (Patrick J. Endres)*

An unforgettable portrait of ancient geology greets visitors to the Graylime Creek area of Gates of the Arctic National Park. (Gil Mull)

FACING PAGE: *A distinctive landmark on the Dalton Highway, Sukakpak Mountain (4,459 feet) is made up of marble of Devonian-age Skajit limestone and graphitic phyllite of probable Paleozoic age. The Paleozoic era extends from about 570 to 245 million years ago; within that time span lies the Devonian period at 408 to 360 million years ago. (Tom Culkin)*

RIGHT: *Far less dramatic than its eastern counterpart, the western Brooks Range consists primarily of weathered hills, mesas and broad valleys. Major deposits of valuable minerals are tucked away in these valleys and this geologist is canvassing the Wulik area for signs of mineralization. The famous Red Dog zinc mine in the DeLong Mountains is among the world's largest. Jointly operated by Cominco Ltd. of Canada and NANA, the regional Native corporation for northwestern Alaska, the mine entered full production in 1991. Zinc concentrate is trucked along a 54-mile road from the mill site to a concentrate storage building at a port near Kivalina on the Chukchi coast. (Bill Sherwonit)*

BELOW RIGHT: *Aufeis, some patches reaching 20 feet high, rests in a channel of the Ivishak River. Aufeis forms as water overruns a frozen section of river and freezes in successive layers. (Gil Mull)*

until we hit bottom. Then we would climb out, push, drag or manhandle the raft in some other way until we got it across a riffle or over to the proper channel, then pile in again. This routine went on for several days. We'd load the raft, paddle, break for lunch and a rest, paddle again, then make camp.

Meanwhile the Brooks Range and its environment passed by, the pillars of Lisburne

For more information on *recreation in the Brooks Range, contact: Gates of the Arctic National Park and Preserve, P.O. Box 74680, Fairbanks, AK 99707; Arctic National Wildlife Refuge, 101 12th Avenue, Box 20, Fairbanks, AK 99701; and Northwest Alaska Areas, National Park Service, P.O. Box 1029, Kotzebue, AK 99752.*

limestone guarding approaches to the valley. One evening a lone caribou crossed the river, ran between members of our group and when it realized it was so close to people, it streaked up the valley. Ptarmigan chortled from the brush skirting the hillsides, American golden plovers flitted across the tundra and semipalmated plovers scurried across the gravel bars.

Several days into the trip we approached the S-curve through which the Hulahula squirts before leaving the mountains and heading out onto the coastal plain. Here I had another one of those experiences that are filed under misadventures in my mind. Our guide had been this way before and knew of the dangerous waters along this stretch. The high water fueled the power of the river through the constricted channel and our guide decided to line the raft

around part of the curve. We could see our intended campsite washed in bright sun on a tundra-blanketed meadow just beyond the last half of the curve. No problem, we thought. We could paddle through this roiling water and be basking in the 80-degree sun in no time. Well, anytime people get too big for their britches, the Brooks Range has a way of serving up a dish of humility. We had no sooner put our backs into paddling through the curve when I went flying off the port side and landed in the middle of the river. "Landed" implies feet first. Not so. I left the raft in a sitting position, entered the water in a sitting position and, amazingly enough, actually sat on a rock about 2 1/2 to 3 feet under the water in the middle of the river. The raft had hung up on the same rock that had propelled me out of the boat. By the time the boat started to swing off the rock, my raftmate on the port side reached out a hand and began to pull me back into the boat. The two paddlers on the starboard side grabbed ahold of whatever part of me they could find, and away we went, now paddling to retrieve the paddle I had lost when I was tossed out. All paddles safely back aboard and the S-curve

behind us, we eased over to the shore and tied the raft up for the night. I climbed out, poured the water out of my boots and checked for damage. There was none. My glasses, hat and inner garments didn't even get wet. Could things have been worse? Certainly. But I figure the Hulahula decided this tenderfoot just wasn't worth keeping. ∎

The Perfect Loop

By Nick Jans

It was one of those moments you have a tough time explaining to yourself, let alone to anyone else. Drenched with sweat, panting, knee-deep in snow, I stood below the crest of Angiaak Pass, on the southern rim of the Noatak Valley. Above me, the granite spires of Igikpak loomed in the arctic twilight. Three miles ahead lay the Kobuk divide, and two miles past that, the precipitous drop into the canyons of the upper Reed River. *[See map, page 6, for route.]*

Maybe I was a little nervous, knowing that the only way home lay down that one-way slope, 150 miles by snowmobile and sled through rough, unknown country. But where I was and where I was headed were clear enough. They were facts that could be measured on maps, weighed on the scales of rationality. Together with my friends Lynn and Carol Norstadt, I'd chosen to be here, and that choice was still fine by me.

Trundling a 55-gallon drum half full of gas up a mountain pass was another matter: 200 awkward, sloshing pounds, wrestled end over

end, 3 feet a whack, hundreds of yards up a rocky, snow-slicked slope. It didn't matter that we needed the drum up there, or that this was the only way to do it. The act itself seemed so damn silly and pointless that it took on a life of its own. The mountains, I suspected, were snickering behind my back.

A half mile below, the whine of a speeding

snow machine cut the silence. I paused to watch as Lynn, driving like a maniac, launched up the hill. Bouncing off rocks, sled fishtailing, engine screaming, he fought for momentum. Carol, a hundred yards to my right, dropped her burden — a pair of 6-gallon fuel jugs, 40 pounds each — to cheer him on. Every yard he gained meant that much less for us to carry. No use. He bogged down and sank in a spray of snow, 50 yards downslope.

Piles of gear and gas cans, maybe 600 pounds in all, lay scattered across the hill, marking the spots where Lynn had ditched a series of loads. From there, we'd mule everything up the last pitch. My brand-new machine — running on one lung, suffering from an alarming, as yet unidentified mechanical crapout — was already at the top, essentially useless for serious pulling. Just over halfway through a 350-mile jaunt through some of the most remote country in Alaska, down to a machine and a half, we were up against trouble.

"Look," Lynn had said back in Ambler, brandishing his USGS 1:250,000 contour map. "It's a loop. You can get up right here, then through there, then down." I peered doubtfully at the fine brown contour lines, each representing a 200-foot change in elevation, compressed, on the map's scale, to about five miles per inch. Where Lynn was pointing — the heart of the Schwatka Mountains, where they straddled the Kobuk-Noatak divide — lines were convoluted

During the return leg of their journey to Ambler, the trio had to be aware of weakening ice that could collapse under the weight of their snow machines. (Bill Sherwonit)

The traditional travel route through the Brooks Range is by way of rivers. Here, the muddy banks of the John River are exposed after a flood in 1994. (Chlaus Lotscher)

as calves' brains, so densely packed you needed a magnifying glass to sort them out. And there, defining one edge of the thread-thin route he proposed, was Igikpak: the tallest peak in the western Brooks Range, 8,510 feet of sawtooth ridges, pinnacles and hanging glaciers. Angiaak Pass, an old Eskimo travel route, lay, quite literally, on the mountain's enormous shoulder.

"Right through here, then down into the Reed, across here into the Beaver, over behind Selby Lake, and from there it's cake. A perfect loop."

Lynn has a thing about loops. The concept is simple enough. You travel away from home, then find a way back without retracing your trail. The Brooks Range, all hundred thousand square miles or so, offers infinite loop opportunities. While I'm all for the basic idea, I have an incredibly strong, somewhat bizarre fixation on traveling well and getting home in one piece.

Unfortunately, the two notions are often at odds. Suffice to say that Lynn's ultimate loop fantasy involves traversing a pass so steep that you have to dismantle your machine, drag it uphill piece by piece, and lower it by ropes on the far side. Judging from the map, Angiaak Pass was a little short of that. But a 200-foot contour map often omits important stuff, 199-foot cliffs, for example. That no one had ever crossed Angiaak with snow machine was a virtual certainty. No one in his right mind would consider it.

Except Lynn, maybe. Five nine, slightly swaybacked, boyish grin and wire rim glasses, he looks exactly like the first-grade teacher he is. Put him out in the country, though, and out comes the relentless drive of a wolverine, and a serious penchant for edgework. Carol's another story. She loves these trips as much as Lynn does, and she's tough enough to ride the runners of a basket sled all day; but she knows where to draw the line. I signed on, counting on her to talk down her husband if things got too crazy.

Nick Jans begins his loop through the Brooks Range from the Inupiat community of Ambler, population 309, on the Kobuk River. (Staff)

Traveling like this, a few hundred miles between phone booths, no AAA or 7-11, is, under the best of conditions, an iffy proposition. In the relatively benign conditions of late March, we could count on 30 below zero, big winds, chest-deep snow, whiteouts, overflow and rotten ice. In the upper Noatak, far off the web of trails between villages, we'd have to bail ourselves out if things went wrong.

Packing and planning took weeks of part-time work, woven around everyday chores and teaching at the Ambler school. We each had brand-new snow machines and solid sleds, but we'd traveled enough to know that was no guarantee against breakdowns. Bags of bolts, tools, patching material and parts were a good part of our load. I've known guys who sometimes carried whole spare engines.

Our shelter was an 8-by-10 canvas wall tent lined with tarps and caribou skins, heated by a sheet metal wood stove, and lit by a Coleman lantern — in a nutshell, pretty identical to the outfit favored a century ago. Our sleeping bags, parkas and coveralls, if somewhat higher tech, were hardly what you'd call expedition gear. Though we shared a combined 20-odd years and thousands of Brooks Range miles, some in severe conditions, this trip was a whole new level in all respects. At least we knew enough to be nervous.

Gas is always the logistical bottleneck on a long snow machine trip. The stuff is heavy: 6 1/2 pounds a gallon. Though a good machine might get up to 18 miles a gallon under perfect conditions, pulling a full sled through deep snow might mean half that. For two machines in mountain country, we decided on roughly 90 gallons. After topping off our tanks, I'd lug

75 gallons on my freight sled — a full drum plus 20 in plastic cans. The good news was that our 600 pounds of gas and oil would get lighter by about a hundred pounds a day.

We set out on March 18, a bright clear morning, 15 below. I'd know the first hundred miles, I thought; 10 years before, I'd traveled as far as the Noatak, tracing a trail left by Eskimo wolf hunters: up the Ambler River, then north up the Redstone to Ivishak (Iviisaaq) Pass, past the treeline into the windswept Cutler Valley, following a series of shortcuts that traversed canyons, wide flats and endless rolling hills, through range upon range of folded white mountains until, quite suddenly, the expanse of the Noatak opened like magic.

By the time we reached Ivishak Pass, just 30 miles from Ambler, dusk was settling in. We'd struggled up the Redstone through soft snow, bogging down again and again, once taking an hour to move a few dozen yards. Now, ahead of us, a huge cloud of windblown snow billowed out of the pass.

Ivishak, on the best of days, is a wind tunnel. What we hit was average — 30 knots, gusting to 40, seven miles of waist-high, rock-hard, sled-flipping drifts. When we finally stood on the rim of the upper Cutler, we'd spent all day and 12 gallons of gas to move less than 40 miles. The wind had eased a little, but the temperature was falling.

Exhausted, our sweat-soaked parkas stiffening, we decided to camp in a narrow side valley that seemed to offer some shelter. Above the treeline now, we guyed the tent to our machines, ate a quick meal, and burrowed into our bags.

The wind slammed in two hours later. I

Fishermen hike the Kugrak Valley, tributary of the Noatak River. (Tom Falley)

awoke with my head outside, face full of snow, wondering what the hell was going on. Despite being tethered to a half ton of machinery, the whole tent was threatening to become airborne.

FACING PAGE: *Mount Igikpak is composed of granite that was originally intruded during the Devonian period, about 380 million years ago. It was uplifted during construction of the present Brooks Range, probably about 90 to 110 million years ago. (Jon R. Nickles)*

BELOW: *Alfred Hulse Brooks (1871-1924) spearheaded U.S. Geological Survey exploration in Alaska for more than two decades. (Historical Photograph Collection, photo no. 83-209-134N, Archives, University of Alaska Fairbanks)*

RIGHT: *The sun returns to this area in the central Brooks Range after a long winter. (Tom Falley)*

The trio bivouacs in a sheltered spot to avoid winds sweeping through the Imelyak Valley. The Imelyak drains northwest slopes of the Schwatka Mountains into the Noatak system. (Nick Jans)

The upwind side, which I'd been lying against, was billowed and snapping like a sail. The three of us had a groggy conference, and decided there was nothing to do but stay in our bags. It was too cold and dark to do much, and the tent seemed to be holding.

I lay there, fighting a rising panic. All our gear was getting plastered with flour-fine snow, and I could feel it melting against the slight warmth of my bag, soaking in. Our parkas and snow pants were already frozen; if our sleeping bags got too wet, we could be in serious trouble. The wind chill had to be a hundred below, and

lighting a stove with the tent jacking around this much was impossible. Lynn later told me he was lying five feet away, thinking the same thing — that, at first light, we needed to throw on our frozen gear and race for home, leaving everything here.

But the wind slowed, then stopped. It had been a terrain-driven squall, one that rose, perhaps, every night. Later on my Eskimo friend Clarence Wood told me we'd been lucky. "Lot of places up there you can't camp. That country around Ivishak is real danger."

After a half day of drying out and warming up, we were back on the trail. We covered another 30 miles before my sled hitch cracked. This time we camped in a sheltered canyon, one of the places Clarence had shown me 10 years ago. Working with a hand drill and angle iron, I patched things up. It was, we all knew, too early for this much crummy luck.

From there, though, the country eased up a little, as if sensing we'd had enough. Despite staggering off course the next day, we pieced together enough between maps and memory to reach the north side of the Noatak. From here on, it would be all new country.

At first we tried traveling up the frozen main river, but wind had stripped most bends of snow. Driving on alternating patches of glare ice and gravel got old fast. Climbing out on the south bank, we found smooth going along the base of the mountains. Except for wrestling sleds through a couple of brushy creek gullies — minor athletic events we dubbed "stuckathons" — we flew up the valley floor, each machine trailing a plume of snow, Carol standing on the sled runners, hanging on, leaning with the turns.

The country was so wide and bright it made your heart ache, enormous sweeps of tundra, mountains rising like great blue-white hands. And every few miles, a new side valley opened like a door, each a separate world beckoning: Nushralatuk, Ipnelivik, Ingning, Kugrak. The absence of trees, of anything familiar to fasten my eyes on, to somehow limit the hugeness, was overwhelming. There was no choice but to let go, and let the country swallow me up.

Out in the middle of all that, without warning, my machine began to falter, one spark plug fouling out and cutting in. It wasn't the plug, though, and everything else seemed fine. I stopped several times to tinker, muttering to myself. To make matters worse, gas was already tight, and now I was using twice as much as I should.

Then, just past the Ingning River, on the edge of a frozen lake, a fuel drum stood. Upright on the ice, almost full, a hundred miles from anyone but us, it seemed a mirage. A pilot, probably a wolf hunter, had cached it weeks before. Someone was counting on it being there. On the other hand, if we didn't take some, we'd be stranded for sure. We settled for six gallons, enough to top off my tank, and went on our way.

As we rounded the Noatak's great southward bend at Portage Creek, Igikpak loomed ahead. Some mountains are huge, and that's about all; Igikpak was a presence, its granite face rising, from this angle, like a slanted, cloud-catching tombstone. We made camp in its shadow, near the mouth of Tupik Creek. Despite my machine, we'd traveled a hundred miles in a single day.

Tomorrow we'd know if Lynn had his loop. If not, we'd be forced to backtrack — which, I let it be known, was fine by me. I wasn't wild about taking a one-lunged rig up there; going back, I argued, was scarcely a retreat. Lynn nodded and unrolled his map. "Look here," he said.

The next thing I knew, I was playing uphill tag with that gas drum, suspecting I was the brunt of some cosmic hoax. There had to be a hidden camera somewhere. But there was only the wind, the mountains, and the sound of my own thumping heart.

Highest point in the western Brooks Range, Mount Igikpak is "8,510 feet of sawtooth ridges, pinnacles and hanging glaciers," in Jans' view. Their route humped over the western shoulder of the peak, taking a trail where no snow machine had ever gone. (Nick Jans)

An overnight bivouac on the crest of Angiaak Pass, though risky, passed without incident, and we were up at first full light. We had to cover at least 50 miles, including that drop into the Reed. Pushed by that sense of urgency, we roared over the pass, Igikpak towering a mile above us, almost unnoticed.

We spent the better part of an hour standing on the far edge, looking down into the canyons of the Reed. Five miles away were the first trees we'd seen since the Redstone, a few wrist-thick spruce. After the barren Noatak, they looked as strange as Martian asparagus.

The trick was the first quarter mile, which seemed almost straight down. Walking back and forth along the rock-strewn rim, we eyed different lines, knowing that we'd have just one chance. We couldn't use brakes or make slalom turns; either meant a jackknifed sled, followed by a long tumble. It was straight down or nothing, and no going back.

Finally we decided. Carol hiked down to check for hidden rocks, and gave the high sign. I shrugged at Lynn and slipped over the edge, chased by four hundred pounds of sled. The canyon floor rushed up at me, rocks blurring past until, in a spray of powder, my sled bottomed out. Far above, Lynn raised his arms. Touchdown.

From here, the trip felt like a record played too fast, as if the freefall down the canyon had never stopped. We knew that even with good luck, we'd need all three days we had left, and the weather was getting warmer by the minute. If the snow collapsed, we'd be stuck. All our energy was focused on traveling. No more gawking at scenery, no leisurely breaks along the trail.

Within a half mile of the pass, we hit our first open water, and barring the way was an irate bull moose. Hackles raised, pawing, he made it clear he wasn't going anywhere. Neither were we, mired in soft snow. Lynn dropped his sled and roared off through the brush, hoping to find a way around. Meanwhile, Carol and I stood behind my sled, shouting, waving, pounding on the drum with a wrench as the moose advanced. Thirty feet out, I fired a warning shot. At 15, I knew he wasn't stopping. There wasn't much choice. We went on our way, feeling pretty glum, though fresh wolf tracks a mile below hinted the carcass wouldn't go to waste.

A windstorm blows through Ivishak Pass, which, according to U.S. Geological Survey records, is named for the Inupiaq word for iron oxide, Iviisaaq. The pass, at 1,500 feet, lies near the east end of the Baird Mountains and connects the Redstone Valley in the Kobuk drainage with the Cutler Valley in the Noatak drainage. (Nick Jans)

The upper Reed was spectacular, but traveling here was like moving down a funnel — deep snow, thick timber, and, everywhere we looked, shaky ice. The river, we knew, was fed by warm springs, and now we knew how many. Sometimes there was no choice but to skip over patches of open water, or trust skimpy ice bridges.

Our next crossover wasn't any better. Akurekvik Pass, which showed on the map low and open, was a tangled mess of brush and black spruce. Our reward for fighting through that was mile after mile of dark, rotten ice on Beaver Creek, where a wrong move would mean a drowned machine. But we always found a way past, navigating by compass, tree climbing and guesswork. There wasn't any choice.

We made our last camp in the thick timber between the Beaver and Narvak Lake. Though we had only 20 miles left before we broke into the open, it was obvious that we didn't have enough gas. My machine could barely pull itself. The last good drive belt, pushed to the limit, had burst into flames the day before.

Sitting on caribou skins around the stove, drying gear cluttered everywhere, we figured our options. We could make it, we thought, if we cached most of our gear, including the tent and stove, right here, along with my sled. Traveling light and fast, both machines should at least carry us within walking distance of Shungnak. Ambler was an hour past that. We'd make a run and worry about details tomorrow.

Twelve hours later, we were in Shungnak, sitting dazed in Raymond Woods's warm, bright cabin, eating chicken, drinking coffee, and trying to explain where we'd been.

This spring, I stand again on the south rim

The Noatak River flows along the south side of the DeLong Mountains on its way to Kotzebue Sound. Lt. George M. Stoney named the mountains for Navy Lt. Cmdr. George W. DeLong, commander of the steamer Jeannette, *who died in Russia's Lena River delta in 1881. (Gil Mull)*

of Angiaak Pass, looking down into the upper Reed. I can almost see the spot where we met the moose. Beyond, the first trees wait. I walk the edge, looking down through the boulders, and once more feel my stomach tighten. Igikpak rises implacable, granite spires dark against the sky. I sit for a while, alone with this place, trying to call back seven years. Somewhere below there must be a canyon, a narrow trail past open water and down through the trees, the one perfect loop that leads me back where I came from. ∎

W. L. Howard

A Pioneering Journey Through the Western Brooks Range

[See map, page 6, for Howard's route.]

When Nick Jans and his companions undertook a wintertime "Perfect Loop" through a portion of the western Brooks Range, they added another link in a chain of exploration that has an illustrious history. As Jans points out, not many white people made cross-country traverses of the western mountains. Among those who did was William Lauriston Howard, a Naval ensign, who crossed from the Kobuk Valley to Barrow in one of the earliest explorations of north-western Alaska's interior. In so doing, he left his name on Alaska's landscape: the Howard Hills of the Brooks Range and Howard Pass between the Noatak and Colville drainages are named for the young explorer.

• • •

Ensign Howard left Fort Cosmos (Shungnak) on the Kobuk River April 12, 1886. His assignment: to travel overland to Point Barrow on the arctic coast. Howard undertook the trek as part of Lt. George M. Stoney's U.S. Naval Exploring Expedition of 1885-86.

Howard, born in Plainfield, Conn., Jan. 10, 1860, was an 1882 graduate of the Naval Academy. He already had some experience in the eastern Arctic when he received word from Stoney inviting him to join the northwestern Alaska efforts. Howard met Stoney in San Francisco and they headed north.

The first part of Howard's route had been explored earlier. The ensign traveled down the Kobuk River to the Ambler River, then up the Ambler to the Redstone. From there, his party ascended the second major tributary entering from the west and reached a pass known as Apkugaagzug to the Natives. This pass is just to the west of Ivishak Pass. Apkugaagzug took them to the headwaters of the Cutler River in the Noatak drainage.

He followed the Cutler downstream to its junction with the Imelyak, where he cut overland to the village of Aneyuk at the junction of the Noatak and Aniuk rivers.

In *The Brooks Range*, Vol. 4, No. 2 of *ALASKA GEOGRAPHIC®*, Edwin S. Hall Jr., who had been researching early exploration in the northern Interior, wrote, "The exact route of the next portion of the journey, from the Noatak to the Colville River is in considerable doubt. Howard sledged from Aneyuk to a village he called Shotcoaluk, which was located up the Noatak River at the mouth of Atongarak Creek. He then cut across country again, heading northeast.

"Shortly after crossing into the Colville drainage, Howard's party reached the village of Tooloouk (Tuluuk), where he was to remain for several days. They then headed down the Nigu River to the Etivluk River and down the latter, in easy stages, to Erivolipar, a village at the confluence of the Etivluk and Colville rivers."

Once on what is now known as the North Slope, Howard continued down the Colville and Ikpikuk rivers to the coast and on to Barrow.

An important result of Howard's journey is the chronicling of the changing culture of the interior Inupiat. The Natives who roamed the mountains and interior valleys year-round were moving to the coast and consolidating their settlements even by the time Howard passed through the country. More than a decade later when the U.S. Geological Survey's F.C. Schrader became the next Outsider to travel this way, the interior cultures that Howard had noted were basically gone. And today, 110 years after Howard's journey, only the Nunamiut of Anaktuvuk Pass carry on the traditions of the Natives of northern Alaska's interior. ■

FACING PAGE: *River runners camp near the confluence of the Noatak and Aniuk rivers, where W.L. Howard spent time 110 years ago before continuing on his journey from Fort Cosmos on the Kobuk River to Point Barrow. (Tom Falley)*

Alaska's Arctic Mountain People

By Chris Wooley

On a three-dimensional map of Alaska, the Brooks Range forms a wrinkled and seemingly impenetrable barrier to the Arctic. Viewed from a small plane, the country seems desolate and forbidding. However, to urban sportsmen, the promise of trophy sheep and lake trout makes the region nearly irresistible. To adventurers, the mountains are a modern Eden far removed from the noise and activity of Western civilization where they can enjoy soaring peaks and diverse ecosystems in relative solitude — a primordial territory that puts them back on even terms with the wilderness.

In the eyes of local residents the mountains are home. The oral history of the region is filled with stories of people who have known the country intimately for many generations. There are fabulous stories of giants, dwarfs, mammoths and other strange beings who inhabited the mountains long ago. There are more recent accounts of successful hunting expeditions followed by great messenger feasts. Some stories recount the sad occasions when caribou did not come through the passes in great numbers and the people starved. Some mention feuds between Inupiat people and their Athabaskan neighbors to the south. There are stories by and about important people named Ahgook, Etalook, Hopson, Hugo, Kakinya, Lincoln, Mekiana, Morry, Paneak, Riley, Rulland and others. Many places in these stories have Inupiat names that are not on published maps. Local residents have a distinctly Inupiat view of both the mountains

LEFT: *Anaktuvuk-style caribou-skin masks, in which the skin is stretched and dried over a wooden face mold, originated in the early 1950s. (Steve McCutcheon)*

FACING PAGE: *Earlier seminomadic Nunamiut moved their camps around the Anaktuvuk River valley, which remains a lush break among the peaks of the Brooks Range. (George Wuerthner)*

When the traditionally nomadic Nunamiut began to settle in the Anaktuvuk Pass area about a half century ago, they first built sod houses to shelter their families. (Steve McCutcheon)

and of the world in general that has been shaped and passed on through the generations.

In political terms, the area is a mosaic of interlocking and sometimes overlapping administrative and management units of state and federal governments, Alaska Native corporations and the North Slope Borough. Recent issues such as local access to subsistence hunting areas, land trades related to natural resource development and efforts to maintain wilderness have elicited divergent views of this remarkable landscape. In the midst of such complexity, the region's Native people try to maintain an important focus — harvesting and sharing food that the land provides.

The village of Anaktuvuk Pass is home for the Inupiat people also known as "the

Nunamiut Eskimo." The term *nunamiut* is a descriptive term that has come to be associated with the Inupiat people from Anaktuvuk Pass. It means, literally, "inland people" as opposed to *tariumiut* or "coastal people." Smithsonian anthropologist E.S. Burch has described how this classification truly applies only to a portion of Northern Alaska; and even then it was only reasonably accurate between about 1885 and 1910. Regardless of their label and no matter what misunderstandings have been caused by

the rapid culture change of the 20th century, the Inupiat people of the Brooks Range are residents of a unique homeland.

Inupiaq-speaking people are the most recent Native residents of the Brooks Range — a region with a 12,000-year legacy of human

The community of Anaktuvuk Pass was less than 20 years old when this photo of villagers walking into town was taken in 1970. (Pete Martin)

occupation. Archaeologists are steadily piecing together the region's pre-European history by excavating key sites and reconstructing the ancient environment. For hundreds of years before European contact, Inupiat groups in the Brooks Range lived a nomadic life based largely on caribou hunting. Band survival depended on expert knowledge of caribou migration routes, caribou behavior, hunting skills and the ability to effectively compile and pass on this knowledge to succeeding generations of hunters. Sheep, wolves, marmots, fish and plants were also important, but caribou-skin garments and shelters were essential.

By 1974 (below), modern houses had only just begun to appear on the Anaktuvuk Pass landscape. About ten years later (right), the modernization trend had expanded to include a new school and a majority of modern houses. (Below, staff; right George Wuerthner)

With the advent of commercial whaling in the Beaufort Sea during the late 1800s and early 1900s, people from the mountains came to the coast to trade and also to obtain work. After the whalers left in the early 1900s, arctic fox trapping attracted many of the remaining inland people to the coast. About the same time, the caribou population crashed, removing the primary food staple of the mountain people and causing great hardship. Non-indigenous disease epidemics spread inland causing widespread depopulation of the Brooks Range. The survivors left the mountains and joined friends and relatives in coastal villages in Alaska and Canada. Some groups of families returned to the mountains in the 1930s and 1940s to reestablish old territories after the coastal fur-trade posts closed and inland caribou populations began to rebound.

The history of Anaktuvuk Pass village is

Jenny Paneak of Anaktuvuk Pass butchers a caribou in the Ekokpuk Valley. (Henry P. Huntington)

the story of Inupiat families who settled permanently in the pass in the 1950s after having reestablished themselves in the region. Contact with bush pilots who brought supplies to the families increased, making long trading trips unnecessary. A trading post was set up in 1949. Sod houses were built and a post

office was established in the village in 1951. Educational opportunities have only been available to residents since a permanent school opened in 1961. In the 1980s and 1990s, North Slope Borough employment opportunities have created additional economic and social changes. Even though life is different than it was when the ancestors of the people were spread across the Brooks Range, families continue to hunt, fish, trap and travel extensively throughout the region. Most importantly, the Inupiat tradition of food sharing persists as a visitor is frequently invited to share meals of caribou, fish or duck soup. Relatives from coastal villages often bring whale meat and blubber (muktuk or maktak) to town, and it is common to see boxes containing wild foodstuffs being packed onto small planes headed to or from Barrow and other regional villages.

Much Inupiat cultural knowledge is encoded in the stories documenting the relationship between people and the land: place names, origin stories, hunting and fishing lore, old campsite recollections. There is a synergetic relationship between place names and tradition. When people know the land intimately, their language and traditions are precise and explicit. Places of importance form the cornerstone of the stories, oral histories and cultural traditions among the Brooks Range Inupiat. The river valleys such as the John, Anaktuvuk, Etivluk, Nigu, Killik,

Okokmilaga, Itkillik and others are named in sharp detail. Lake and trail systems provide access to caribou migration routes, sheep hunting sites and fish camps. The human history of the region is reflected in the cultural geography and in stories told about the important events that occurred at each site.

Current Anaktuvuk Pass residents are benefactors of the preceding generations' ability to understand and adapt to an ever-changing environment, fluctuating game populations and migration habits, and human group migrations. They have survived pervasive 19th- and 20th-century epidemics and more recent social changes engendered by resource industrialization, Alaska statehood and the passage of the Alaska Native Claims Settlement Act. Contemporary residents are quick to tell anthropologists and other visitors that the inland Inupiat culture remains strong and active. They want outsiders to respect their unique status and understand that history, language and culture have molded their current relationship to the land.

America's image of the Arctic remains vague, and Western visitors tend to worship the natural beauty of the land and its wildlife. Some may be put off by Native hunters using snow machines, ATVs and rifles to hunt for food. Yet, from the village perspective, these items are merely the best tools to use to obtain and share food. When the satisfaction of

feeding one's family and friends is the goal, tool types are irrelevant. Adventurers may yearn for pristine, untouched wilderness, but the reality is that the Brooks Range is both a natural landscape where visitors can get close to nature, and a cultural landscape dotted with ancient and modern campsites, kill sites, trails and places where giants once walked. The Brooks Range landscape is rugged and beautiful, yet it is also a peoples' homeland imbued with deep historical and cultural meaning. ■

Nunamiut celebrate 4th of July in 1975. In 1996 about 280 people lived in the settlement nestled in the broad pass between the headwaters of the John and Anaktuvuk rivers. (Gil Mull)

Bibliography

Several *ALASKA GEOGRAPHIC*® titles contain detailed knowledge of portions of the Brooks Range, including:

Alaska's Oil/Gas & Minerals Industry, Vol. 9, No. 4, 1982.
Up The Koyukuk, Vol. 10, No. 4, 1983
Arctic National Wildlife Refuge, Vol. 20, No. 3, 1993
Prehistoric Alaska, Vol. 21, No. 4, 1994.
Rich Earth, Vol. 22, No. 3, 1995

Jans, Nick. *The Last Light Breaking*. Portland and Seattle: Graphic Arts Center Publishing, 1994.

—. *A Place Beyond*. Portland and Seattle: Graphic Arts Center Publishing, 1996.

Kauffmann, John M. *Alaska's Brooks Range, The Ultimate Mountains*. Seattle: The Mountaineers, 1992.

Mull, C.E. and K.E. Adams, eds. *Dalton Highway, Yukon River to Prudhoe Bay, Alaska*. Vols. 1 and 2. Fairbanks: State of Alaska, Division of Geological & Geophysical Surveys, 1989.

Simmerman, Nancy Lange. *Alaska's Parklands, The Complete Guide*. Seattle: The Mountaineers, 1983.

Thorson, Robert M.; Jean S. Aigner; R. Dale and Mary Lee Guthrie; William S. Schneider and Richard K. Nelson. *Interior Alaska, A Journey Through Time*. Anchorage: The Alaska Geographic Society, 1986.

U.S. Department of the Interior. *Arctic National Wildlife Refuge, Alaska, Coastal Plain Resource Assessment, Vols. 1 and 2*. Washington D.C.: U.S. Department of the Interior, 1987.

U.S. Fish and Wildlife Service. *Alaska Maritime National Wildlife Refuge, Comprehensive Conservation Plan, Environmental Impact Statement, Wilderness Review, Final Summary*. Anchorage: U.S. Fish and Wildlife Service, 1988.

—. *Arctic National Wildlife Refuge, Comprehensive Conservation Plan, Environmental Impact Statement, Wilderness Review, Wild River Plans, Final Summary*. Anchorage: U.S. Fish and Wildlife Service, 1988.

Editor's note: *A resident of Juneau and science columnist for the* Los Angeles Times, *Lee Dye last reported on the Juneau Icefield Research Project for ALASKA GEOGRAPHIC®.*

If the Creator was tired when he made the Yukon, as poet Robert W. Service suggests, He must have been cranky when He carved the classic fiord known as Tracy Arm.

Winding through the tortured rocks of the Coast Mountains 50 miles south of Juneau, Tracy Arm is Alaska's other Glacier Bay, less known than the national park about 100 miles to the northwest, but far more intimate. The sheer rock cliffs that line its shores are remnants of some of nature's most violent acts, thrust up from far below the surface as the North American continent bullied its way up over the seafloor to the west.

Left in the wake of that violence millions of years ago was a jumble of rock formations that must have looked a little like a pile of colorful clay, squashed together in anger. Tracy Arm knifes through the rocks like a gorge carved by a finger dragged through icing on a cake.

Easily accessible by day-long excursions out of Juneau, Tracy

Tracy Arm

By Lee Dye // Photos by Pat Costello

Arm is the glacier bay of choice for many who prefer it over Glacier Bay National Park.

"It's neat to have those fiord walls so close," says Cathy Connor, assistant professor of geology at the University of Alaska, Southeast.

So close, in fact, that cruise boats can literally dip their bows under the foot of a cascading waterfall without fear of running aground. The water depth along some of the steep walls is around 1,000 feet.

The rugged terrain is difficult even for mountain goats, which can be seen from time to time clinging to the walls like bugs stuck to a sheet of flypaper. Few other creatures make this their home, save for harbor seals that clamber atop the huge icebergs shed by North Sawyer and South Sawyer glaciers at the end of the fiord, and black-legged kittiwakes and arctic terns that soar along the face of the glaciers.

The Carpe Diem *cruises Tracy Arm. The 30-mile arm lies within the 653,000-acre Tracy Arm-Fords Terror Wilderness Area of Tongass National Forest. Tracy Arm, neighboring Endicott Arm and the Chuck River area received about 100,000 visitors in 1996, most of whom arrived by boat.*

Glacier ice develops in stages. First snow accumulates and evolves into a material called firn, the name given to snow that has endured one summer melt season. This material then changes into glacier ice, when it becomes impermeable to air and water. When the snow accumulates, the lower layers are under increasing pressure, which alters the density, volume and crystal structure of the snow. As snow becomes ice, its volume may decrease by as much as nine times. The blue visible in glacier ice occurs because the physical characteristics of water molecules absorb all colors except blue, which is reflected.

The fiord itself, and the glaciers that carved it, are the show stoppers here.

Tracy Arm has bedeviled geologists for years because it offers one of the clearest examples of how glaciers reshape the landscape, but its geological history is muddied indeed. The easiest part of the story to understand is the glaciation itself. Classic U-shaped valleys, carved by the gradual retreat of glacial arms, attest to the basic force at work here. As the arms retreated, they scoured out the floors of the valleys and left sheer walls with high waterfalls so typical of glacial carving.

A fish finder aboard a small boat can reveal subsurface glacial deposits caused by the last surge of the glaciers more than two centuries ago. The most prominent of these is a massive sandbar across the entrance to Tracy Arm, which can be hazardous to boaters who do not have a keen understanding of the depth of water and the shifting currents.

But the history of Tracy Arm, and how it came to be, is more than just the story of the glaciers moving across the land. It is told in the rocks that were crushed and carved by the massive sheets of ice, and those rocks tell a complicated story.

Lance Miller, a geologist with Echo Bay Mines in Juneau and

Capt. Peter Hanke explores Tracy Arm in one of several cruise ships that offer day excursions from Juneau to the arm. It takes two to four hours to reach the arm, depending on the speed of the boat.

an expert on the Coast Mountains, says early geologists attempted to date the various rock formations around the turn of the century. Although they did not have the advantage of the instruments available to geologists today, they were remarkably accurate in their findings.

"The old timers had a lot of it nailed," Miller says.

By examining such things as the fossil record and the

composition and structure of various rocks, the early geologists determined that the age of the rocks varied greatly throughout the region.

But their finding was originally as confusing as it was illuminating.

Throughout Southeast Alaska, rocks of the same age generally trend in northwesterly patterns, and visitors can see this today in a trip up Tracy Arm. The nature of the formations range from the

The Adventure Bound *appears overwhelmed by the face of North Sawyer Glacier.*

Although it has been retreating in recent years, South Sawyer Glacier still maintains an imposing presence at the head of Tracy Arm. Studies done in the 1980s indicated that the glacier was about 20 miles long and covered an area of about 100 square miles.

green metamorphosed volcanic rocks seen just inside the entrance, to the stark gray walls of the main straightaway of the arm, to the tall granite peaks above the glaciers.

"If you were doing this logically, the youngest rocks should be on the coast and the oldest rocks should be inland," says UA's Connor, because the seafloor is younger than the continent.

But what the old-timers found was that some of the inland rocks are much younger than the coastal rocks. Miller says the so-called Taku Terrane at the mouth of the arm is made up of volcanic sediments that formed in ocean basins on the order of 200 million years ago. Inland of that formation is the Yukon Tanana Terrane, consisting of quartz and sand that washed down from inland mountains 500 to 200 million years ago. But just inland of that lie the much younger Tonalite Sills, formed by molten rock intruding into surface rocks 70 to 50 million years ago. That formation comprises the Coast Mountains batholith, a massive stretch of molten rock that cooled below ground and formed the basement for mountains that stretch from Skagway to Washington.

The question of why younger rocks would be inland of older rocks left geologists "scratching their heads" for years, Connor says. The answer turned the world of geology upside down and forever altered our understanding of the major forces that have shaped our planet.

The solution lies in plate tectonics, and Tracy Arm offers about as good a view of this complex process as any place in the world. The mountains through which the fiord runs were created by rocks that were uplifted as the west coast of North America slid up over the crustal slab that lies under the Pacific Ocean. That process plastered island volcanoes along the coast, some of which may have formed as far away as Australia. Meanwhile, a few miles inland, molten rocks intruded toward the surface, where they cooled into hard rock and rode westward over older sediments.

A few million years ago the game plan shifted, and instead of one plate riding up over another, the two plates began to slide horizontally against each other, causing earthquake faults to ripple through the rocks.

Some of those faults created weaknesses in the surface that helped the glaciers carve deeply into the rocks. Other faults allowed fluids to flow through the rocks, capturing such things as gold. Along the Chuck River at Windham Bay, just over the hill from the mouth of Tracy Arm, prospectors made one of the earliest discoveries of gold in Southeast.

The ancient faults are no longer active. Today, Tracy Arm is a serene place. Even the calving from the two glaciers, which produces some of the largest icebergs in the state, seems calm compared to the violent activity of the past.

"That's why we have all this beautiful geography in western North America," says Miller. "Because of the dynamics that have gone on."

That violent history faded into the distant past one warm summer day as Peter Hanke guided the excursion boat *Sit Ku* (Tlingit for "among the glaciers") up to South Sawyer's

BELOW: *About 100 harbor seals rely on the safety of ice floes in Tracy Arm to have their pups.*

RIGHT: *In addition to mountain goats and harbor seals, black bears and bald eagles are regularly seen in Tracy Arm and humpback, and to a lesser extent killer, whales are common in waters near the arm's entrance. Lt. Cmdr. H.B. Mansfield of the U.S. Navy named the fiord in 1889 for B.F. Tracy, secretary of the Navy under Benjamin Harrison.*

jagged toe, towering several hundred feet above the green waters of Tracy Arm. Harbor seals eyed the vessel curiously as they lounged on icebergs, finding security in a cold home to raise their young. An arctic tern, interrupting its migration of thousands of miles, screamed a protest.

But aboard the boat, there was only hushed silence, an unspoken reverence for the awesome power of nature. ●

Return of the Salmon

By Lee Dye
Photos courtesy of National Marine Fisheries Service, Auke Bay Laboratory

Nature offers few pageants as moving as the return of the salmon to the stream in which its life began, where it will spawn and die in the final epoch of its extraordinary life. This annual ritual is the stuff of legends, and it can be witnessed from the banks of almost any river along the coast of Alaska during the spawning season.

For decades scientists have tried to unravel the secrets of the salmon. Why do these large fish find it so imperative to return to the same stream where they were born to produce their young? And how do they find their way home after traveling thousands of miles through the Gulf of Alaska and the North Pacific Ocean?

The annual return of the salmon is punctuated with myths resulting from an inexplicable human inclination to embellish a story that is already grand. Salmon are not always as faithful to their natal stream as the storytellers would have it, and that's fortunate because in some cases when they return the stream may no longer be there, or a new stream may offer a richer bed in which to produce their young.

Yet their fidelity can be astounding.

"There are more unknowns than knowns," says William Heard, a fisheries biologist with the National Marine Fisheries Service's Auke Bay Laboratory in Juneau. But he adds that much has been learned in recent years, and the salmon is slowly giving up its secrets.

The lab is perched on the bank of Auke Creek, a small stream just a little longer than a football field that is within view of Mendenhall Glacier. In a good year, 20,000 salmon may come home to Auke Creek to reproduce and die. It is from that crystal-clear creek that scientists have extracted some of their most surprising answers.

Fisheries geneticist A. J. (Tony) Gharrett and salmon biologist William W. Smoker of the University of Alaska's School of Fisheries and Ocean Sciences in Juneau have found that the salmon that spawn in Auke Creek are amazingly faithful to their natal stream.

The two scientists used a genetic marker, somewhat like a blood group, to distinguish young Auke Creek salmon from others in the area. Eighteen months later, when the fish returned from the sea, the scientists were able to determine if some had strayed into other streams.

LEFT: *Pink salmon, male above, develop a hump on the back when they return to fresh water after being at sea. They are sometimes referred to as humpback salmon.*

RIGHT: *Chum salmon, also known as dog salmon, have the largest natural distribution of any of North America's Pacific salmon species, from California north around the coast to the Mackenzie delta in the Canadian Arctic.*

To the surprise of many of their colleagues, they found that the marked fish returned only to Auke Creek.

"They spawned at almost exactly the same spot" where they had been born, says Gharrett, and they returned at precisely the same time of the year. "There's an inheritable component for timing," Gharrett says, and "it is passed on from generation to generation."

The Auke Creek salmon did not even stray into a similar stream that is only half a mile away.

Why such faithfulness? Gharrett and Smoker think the salmon that begin their lives in Auke Creek know that their offspring will have a better chance of survival if they return to the same place. Even such things as the size of the pebbles in the creek bed can influence survival rates, because the new eggs are genetically conditioned to cling to pebbles of a certain size. They may simply wash past a sandier bottom and back out to sea, for example. Other factors, such as temperature and natural chemicals in the water, can also influence survival rates.

Auke Creek is also an exceptionally stable stream. Many generations of salmon have spawned there and the collective memory of all those families would have nothing to suggest that the stream may not be there when they return.

So the reproductive odds are better for the salmon of Auke Creek if they return to their birthplace, the scientists say, and the salmon apparently know that.

Such fidelity, however, is not always the case. Elsewhere in Alaska, salmon are believed to return to the same area to spawn, but not necessarily to the same

ABOVE: *Workers clean salmon carcasses off the front of the weir at Auke Creek near Juneau.*

RIGHT: *Sockeye salmon smolt are measured before being released. The adipose fin has been removed from the back to mark these fish. The missing fin indicates that a coded microwire tag has been inserted near the snout. The tag is recovered when the fish reach adulthood.*

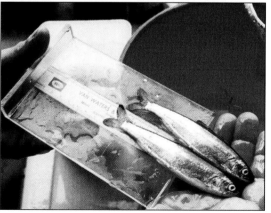

stream. New streams exposed by receding glaciers in Southeast Alaska's Glacier Bay are being recolonized by salmon within 10 years, so some salmon are obviously straying into the new creeks.

Scientists believe that in some areas,

such as earthquake-prone Prince William Sound, streams are less stable than Auke Creek. It may be that salmon born in the creeks along Prince William Sound may instinctively know that their particular stream may not be there when they return, and thus some straying is essential to survival.

No one knows that for certain, however. It is, as Smoker put it, "armchair biology."

The fact that scientists do not know all the intimate details should not be surprising. Only in recent years have they begun to understand how salmon know when to return, and how they find their way home from hundreds of miles away.

Auke Creek, for example, produces one of five types of Pacific salmon, known as the "pink" or "humpy." The pink has a two-year life cycle, and is the most abundant salmon in the ocean.

After spending their first winter in the fresh water of the creek, young salmon emerge in the spring when the sea water is warm enough to provide the nutrients they need for growth. They travel out into the Gulf of Alaska, where they mature into adults.

In the summer of the following year, somehow they know it is time to head back. "The cue that it's time to go home is probably day length," says Smoker. "As the days start to get shorter, they leave off feeding and return to the spawning streams."

Initially, they are guided by the Earth's magnetic field, and possibly by the direction of the morning sun, scientists believe. But that only tells them the general direction in which to head.

They probably use physical clues — literally the lay of the land — to home in closer to their stream, but that still would not tell them which stream is theirs. Many streams in Alaska would appear similar, even to a salmon.

Scientists had puzzled over that for years until pioneering experiments by biologists at the University of Wisconsin provided the answer. Scientists there theorized that salmon were able to detect subtle differences in the odor of different streams. They literally stuffed wads of cotton into the noses of a few salmon and let them go in Puget Sound. The fish became hopelessly lost.

Genetics Aids Fisheries Research

By Lee Dye

Of all the tools available to scientists who want to understand the homing instincts of salmon, none is more powerful than genetics. That rapidly growing field gave scientists their first real opportunity to conduct reliable, large-scale tests of salmon fidelity.

A. J. (Tony) Gharrett and William W. Smoker of the University of Alaska's School of Fisheries and Ocean Sciences have used a genetic marker to determine the fidelity of the pink salmon that spawn in Auke Creek near Juneau. The process is similar to blood grouping in which the blood from one stock will differ from that of another.

The scientists clipped the fins on 180,000 fry released into Auke Creek that carried a specific genetic marker — a blood group — so they would be able to determine which fish to analyze after they returned to Auke Creek or neighboring streams.

"We got back over 1,000 fish that had a fin mark," Gharrett says, and genetic studies showed that the Auke Creek fry had been surprisingly faithful to their natal stream. None were found in nearby streams.

Genetic marking is a vast improvement over previous techniques, such as fish-scale monitoring. Fish scales have circular patterns that are similar to tree rings. The patterns vary according to growth, widespread during periods of high growth and close together during winter seasons when growth is less.

Since fish scales offer clues as to the size of the river from which the salmon came — based on the rate of growth — that permitted scientists to determine whether fish taken in the high seas were likely to have come from a single river. If they all came from the same river, the entire stock could be wiped out, so fish-scale monitoring has been useful for harvest managers who need to know when a stock is in danger of overfishing.

However, fish-scale monitoring alone will not tell which of two similar rivers produced a specific fish, and thus it has not been as helpful in studying the homing instincts of salmon. Genetics is far more precise, allowing scientists to determine if a single salmon has indeed made it home. ●

TOP: *Workers inspect a sample of gravel from a salmon spawning bed to determine how many eggs are buried in a given area and what portion of the eggs are alive.*

ABOVE: *A scientist examines juvenile chinook salmon from individual family matings in small rearing containers to learn if disease organisms are passed from parent to offspring.*

ABOVE RIGHT: *In a study currently in progress, scientists incubate salmon eggs in plastic cups. The eggs have been exposed to gravel that has been coated with different dosages of Prudhoe Bay oil to determine whether and how much low doses of oil influence the homing ability of salmon.*

"It turned out that fish have an extremely high level of olfactory acuity," says Heard. "They make a dog look like he doesn't have a nose. It is extremely powerful."

That sense of smell allows the returning salmon to find the stream that has chemical and biological odors that are the most similar to the one in which its life began.

Gharrett says he has seen that process at work.

"They stick their nose up a lot of different streams before they actually pick a stream to spawn in," he says. Sometimes a salmon will travel a considerable distance up a stream before deciding it is the wrong one and pulling out to find a better prospect, he says.

Scientists believe that most of the time the salmon succeeds. It returns to the same stream, and in the case of Auke Creek, to the same spot at the same time of the year as its own life began. There it spawns and dies, the long, tortured journey finally at an end. ●

Icebox Orchids

By Downs Matthews

Editor's note: *When not chasing walrus, arctic fox and other northern mammals, free-lance writer Downs Matthews steps carefully, checking his path for orchids and other natural wonders.*

Most people know of Alaska's scenic splendors. Few know that the Great Land also hosts wild native orchids.

Orchids in Alaska? How can orchids live in such a cold climate? That's hard to believe.

But it's true. In fact, so hardy are they that every climate zone on earth, with the exception of Antarctica, has its native orchids. Of the 210 species of wild orchids found in the United States and Canada, 31 grow in Alaska, and nine grow north of the Arctic Circle. Obviously, some of the world's 30,000 orchid species have adapted well to cold habitats.

A Word to the Wise

If you should find orchids in flower in Alaska, don't pick them. It's against the law. Nor should you transplant them. Most ground-growing orchids are extremely sensitive to their habitat. The orchids have a dependent relationship with certain kinds of fungi that grow in the soil and will grow nowhere else. Out of its habitat, the plant dies.

◁ Cypripedium passerinum, *northern lady's-slipper. (Verna Pratt)*

Calypso bulbosa var. americana

As soon as nighttime temperatures creep reliably above freezing, the first of Alaska's orchids comes into bloom. *Calypso bulbosa* is its name. *Calypso* was the sea nymph who kept Ulysses captive on her private island. The species name, *bulbosa*, calls attention to the plant's bulbous corm, which is a fat root at the base of the plant where nutrients are stored. Dena'ina Athabaskans of Southcentral Alaska used to harvest *Calypsos* in the spring and eat the nourishing corms as a tasty salad. Ojibway Indians from the Michigan area used their flowers as a love charm.

From mid-May to mid-June, you can see *Calypsos* in huge numbers in the Matanuska Valley, where these fairy slippers pop up on the hillsides all the way to Matanuska Glacier. You'll find them usually in large clusters, sometimes of several hundred flowers, occupying microclimates that meet their unique needs. They like moist humus sheltered by thickets of spruce and poplar into which a little sunshine filters. The ground level temperature at the base of a cluster might be 53

degrees, but a thermometer pushed 2 or 3 inches into the soil will register 40 degrees.

With its dark pink petals and sepals and prominent pink-and-white lip striped in red, this orchid is certainly showy. If not pollinated by flies, mosquitoes or bees, or if not burned up in forest fires, *Calypso* will bloom for about a month.

Corallorhiza trifida

Following the *Calypso* into bloom by just a few days is the distinctive *Corallorhiza* (meaning coralroot) *trifida*. The species name, *trifida*, means "three-lobed" in Latin. The description refers to a pair of small, tooth-shaped lobes found at the base of the flower's lip. *Trifida* occurs in Southeast amid the dense spruce and hemlock forests of that wet region. When your tour ship stops at Ketchikan, Sitka or Yakutat, escape into the surrounding woods and search the moist, shady forest floor. Look for stalks standing about ankle-high topped with yellow-green flowers.

Calypso bulbosa *var.* americana, ▷ *fairy slipper. (Verna Pratt)*

Corallorhiza mertensiana

While you search for *trifida*, look out for its cousin, *mertensiana*, which was named for a German botanist, Franz Carl Mertens. This orchid really looks like the coral that gave the *Corallorhiza* genus its name. It has stalks and flowers of a bright coral red. *Mertensiana* tends to grow in colonies, so if you see one, you're likely to see quite a few.

Cypripediums

While you are in Alaska, be sure to look for a couple of the

five different *Cypripediums* that can be found in the state, depending on where you are. The word *cypripedium* was coined from two Greek words: Cyprus and *pedium*. Cyprus was a goddess of love born on the island of Cyprus. Her specialty was so popular that in the 19th century, Cyprian became a euphemism for prostitute. *Pedium* translates as "little foot," referring to the characteristic pouch. So we get this pretty hooker with size four tootsies, the well-known lady's-slipper orchid.

Cypripedium guttatum

Throughout most of mainland Alaska and quite commonly around Anchorage, you may find the spectacular *Cypripedium guttatum*. In Latin *guttatum* means speckled or spotted. So we get the pink spotted lady's-slipper, known as the pink lady's-slipper.

Guttatum can have a bloomspike up to 12 inches tall. Its single flower is basically white with irregular cranberry red blotches, especially on the petals. The large, bucket-shaped pouch is white on the inside, red on the outside. The dorsal sepal, the one in the middle

◁ Cypripedium guttatum, *pink lady's-slipper. (Jon R. Nickles)*

over the pouch, is white on the back, red on the front. It likes moist meadows and forested hillsides and often grows in colonies of hundreds.

Cypripedium passerinum

If you find yourself between Fairbanks and Anchorage, look for the little sparrow's egg orchid, also called the northern lady's-slipper. The species name *passerinum* translates from the Latin as "sparrow," whose white egg it resembles. The bloomspike rises perhaps 10 inches to produce a single flower about an inch-and-a-half wide with a greenish-white pouch closely framed by green petals and sepals. One orchid scholar, Dr. Claire Ossian, says it looks like a green snake trying to swallow a large white egg. The sparrow's egg orchid starts blooming in late June in wet meadows. Where you find one *passerinum*, you will usually find large colonies, so scout about a bit.

Amerorchis rotundifolia

Should you go to Denali National Park, look about on the wet forest floor there for *Amerorchis rotundifolia*. This name translates loosely as the American round-leafed orchid with the big cojones. It flourishes throughout the Interior in soggy tundra and woodland bogs, and is popularly known as the small round-leafed orchid or the fly-specked orchid. White with red to purple spots are its colors.

The petals and sepals stick out like small wings on either side of the large, three-lobed lip. Bloomspikes run about 6 inches tall, with one leaf, round and flat against the ground.

Dactylorhiza aristata

Should you go to Prince William Sound, the Aleutians or to Kodiak, keep an eye open in July for *Dactylorhiza aristata*. The genus name translates from the Greek as "finger root," referring to the plant's hand-shaped root. The species name, *aristata*, is Latin and calls attention to the slender-pointed petals of the flower. Thus you get the orchid with the fingerlike roots and pointy flowers.

Aristata is not common, but neither is it hard to see. The bloomspikes are usually 8 to 12 inches tall, rising to 18 inches. At the top you'll see clumps of up to 30 flowers that are red enough to stop traffic. Locally, they are called the rose-purple orchid, but some forms are a lighter rose with red stripes and spots. They like open meadows and are often seen with blue lupines.

Listera cordata

When you hike the trails in Southcentral or Southeast, and pass through dark, soggy forests of tamarack and spruce, watch

Dactylorhiza aristata, *rose-* ▷ *purple orchid. (Verna Pratt)*

for areas where fallen timber, moss and tree leaves have made a thick humus on the floor. If you see a pair of heart-shaped leaves, you may have found the widespread *Listera cordata*, perhaps Alaska's most common orchid. The genus *Listera* was named for an English naturalist; the species name, *cordata*, describes its heart-shaped leaves.

Cordata 's common name is heart-leaf twayblade, with twayblade referring to its two leaves. The stem is slender and the flowers quite small, less than an inch wide, and varying in color from green to brown.

◁ Listera cordata, *heart-leaf twayblade. (Jon R. Nickles)*

Platanthera

The genus *Platanthera* has several Alaskan representatives. *Platanthera*, in Greek, means a wide anther, the organ inside the lip where the flower's pollen is stored. Three that you may see in Alaska are *dilatata*, *hyperborea* and *obtusata*.

Platanthera dilatata

You'll find *Platanthera dilatata* in the marine climate zones of Southcentral and Southeast, usually in full bloom by June 15. This is an elegant plant with wide leaves from which a long, slender bloomspike grows straight up like an asparagus stalk. At the summit, up to 50 small, white blooms appear, arranged like the seeds of an ear of corn. The name *dilatata* refers to the widened or dilated base of the lip. This species smells strongly of cloves and is commonly called the white bog orchid, because it likes its feet wet.

If you should drive to Denali National Park in late June or July, watch for huge stands of *dilatata* alongside the road.

More on Alaska Orchids

Here are sources of information to help you organize your search for Alaska orchids.

• **Reference books:** *Native Orchids of the United States and* Alaska, Excluding Florida, by Carlyle Luer, New York Botanical Garden; *Flora of Alaska and Neighboring Territories,* by Eric Hulten, Stanford University Press.

• **Field guides:** *Alaskan Wildflowers,* by Dr. Verna E. Pratt, self-published; *Alaska-Yukon Wild Flowers Guide,* Alaska Northwest Publishing Co.; *Barrenland Beauties,* by Page Burt, Outcrop, Limited.

• **Field trips:** For a day's walking tour to see wildflowers in and around Anchorage, write Dr. Verna Pratt, 7446 East 20th Avenue, Anchorage, AK 99504, or call (907) 333-8212. For a longer, wider-ranging tour, write Paul Martin Brown, P. O. Box 759, Acton, ME 04001-0759, May through October, or 15 Dresden St., Jamaica Plain, MA 02130-4407, November through April.

• **Organizations:** (1) The American Orchid Society, 6000 South Olive Avenue, West Palm Beach, FL 33405-4199, (407) 585-8666; (2) The Alaskan Orchid Society, 1300 West 47th Avenue, Anchorage, AK 99503, (907) 561-7991; (3) The North American Native Orchid Alliance, 84 Etna St., Brighton, MA 02135

• **Periodicals:** *Orchids,* published by the American Orchid Society; the *North American Native Orchid Journal,* published by the North American Native Orchid Alliance.

—Downs Matthews

◁ Platanthera dilatata. *(Verna Pratt)*

Spiranthes romanzoffiana, ▷ *hooded ladies' tresses. (Jon R. Nickles)*

Platanthera hyperborea

Dilatata's Yankee cousin, *Platanthera hyperborea* is the *Platanthera* that grows up north, which is what *hyperborea* means. It blooms about the same time as *dilatata*, in the latter half of June. The flowers resemble those of *dilatata*, greenish white and sometimes greenish yellow in color. Look for them in the Interior wherever you find a muskeg or a bog with standing water. Other names for *hyperborea* are the northern green bog orchid and the green-flowered bog orchid.

Platanthera obtusata

Almost anywhere else in Alaska but the far North, you stand a chance of finding *Platanthera obtusata*. The species name calls attention to the rounded, or blunt, ends of the plant's leaves. It is a champion bloomer, bringing out its yellow-green flowers on 6-inch spikes from June to September. Its popular name is the small northern bog orchid, which indicates that you should look for it when you find soft, wet ground.

Spiranthes romanzoffiana

You may find this handsome orchid almost anywhere in Alaska south of the Brooks Range, or for that matter, anywhere in northern North America. The genus name comes from Greek words meaning coils of flowers; the

species was named for Russian diplomat Nicholas Romanzoff. In perfect symmetry, the creamy-white flowers ascend the bloomspike in neat, orderly spirals. One botanist described the flower as resembling a face with a receding chin, but it is better known by its popular name of hooded ladies' tresses, which calls to mind braids of hair. It's a late bloomer, appearing from late July and to early August.●

◁ Calypso bulbosa, *fairy slipper. (Jon R. Nickles)*

Checklist of the Orchids of Alaska

Compiled by Paul Martin Brown, 1996

1. SMALL ROUND-LEAVED ORCHIS, *Amerorchis rotundifolia*

2. EASTERN FAIRY-SLIPPER, *Calypso bulbosa* var. *americana*

2a. WESTERN FAIRY-SLIPPER, *Calypso bulbosa* var. *occidentalis*

3. NORTHERN BRACTED GREEN ORCHIS, *Coeloglossum viride*

3a. LONG BRACTED GREEN ORCHIS, *Coeloglossum viride* var. *virescens*

4. WESTERN CORALROOT, *Corallorhiza mertensiana*

5. EARLY CORALROOT, *Corallorhiza trifida*

6. SPOTTED LADY'S-SLIPPER, *Cypripedium guttatum*

7. MOUNTAIN LADY'S-SLIPPER, *Cypripedium montanum*

8. LARGE YELLOW LADY'S-SLIPPER, *Cypripedium parviflorum* var. *pubescens*

9. SPARROW'S EGG LADY'S-SLIPPER, *Cypripedium passerinum* var. *passerinum*

10. YELLOW SPOTTED LADY'S-SLIPPER, *Cypripedium yatabeanum* var. *yatabeanum*

10a. ALASKAN SPOTTED LADY'S-SLIPPER, *Cypripedium xalaskanum*

11. FISCHER'S ORCHID, *Dactylorhiza aristata* var. *aristata*

11a. KODIAK ORCHID, *Dactylorhiza aristata* var. *kodiakensis*

12. GIANT RATTLESNAKE ORCHIS, *Goodyera oblongifolia*

13. LESSER RATTLESNAKE ORCHIS, *Goodyera repens*

14. NORTHERN TWAYBLADE, *Listera borealis*

15. NORTHWESTERN TWAYBLADE, *Listera caurina*

16. BROAD-LIPPED TWAYBLADE, *Listera convallarioides*

17. WESTERN HEART-LEAVED TWAYBLADE, *Listera cordata* var. *nephrophylla*

18. WHITE ADDER'S MOUTH, *Malaxis brachypoda*

19. TWO-LEAVED ADDER'S MOUTH, *Malaxis monophyllos* var. *diphyllos*

20. BOG ADDER'S MOUTH, *Hammarbya paludosa*

21. SLENDER WHITE PIPERIA, *Piperia candida*

22. ALASKA PIPERIA, *Piperia unalascensis*

23. CHAMISSO'S ORCHID, *Platanthera chorisiana*

24. TALL WHITE NORTHERN BOG ORCHIS, *Platanthera dilatata* var. *dilatata*

24a. BOG CANDLES, *Platanthera dilatata* var. *albiflora*

24b. SIERRA REIN ORCHIS, *Platanthera dilatata* var. *leucostachys*

25. GREEN BOG ORCHIS, *Platanthera huronensis*

26. NORTHERN GREEN BOG ORCHIS, *Platanthera hyperborea* var. *hyperborea*

26a. LAXLY FLOWERED BOG ORCHIS, *Platanthera hyperborea* var. *gracilis*

26b. TALL ALASKA GREEN ORCHIS, *Platanthera hyperborea* var. *viridiflora*

27. BLUNT-LEAVED REIN ORCHIS, *Platanthera obtusata*

28. PAD-LEAVED ORCHIS, *Platanthera orbiculata*

29. SLENDER BOG ORCHIS, *Platanthera stricta*

30. BEHRING ORCHIS, *Platanthera tipuloides*

30a. CORRELL'S REIN ORCHIS, *Platanthera xcorrellii*

30b. ESTES REIN ORCHIS, *Platanthera xestesii*

30c. INTERMEDIATE REIN ORCHIS, *Platanthera xmedia*

31. HOODED LADIES' TRESSES, *Spiranthes romanzoffiana* ●

News and Reviews

A number of intriguing books have reached *ALASKA GEOGRAPHIC*® headquarters in recent months, some light-hearted, some comprehensive, but all sporting a "Suitable for Giving" button.

Outhouses of Alaska.

Harry M. Walker. Epicenter Press, Box 82368, Kenmore, WA 98028. 64 pages; 120 color photos; hardcover, $14.95, add $3 for priority mail shipping.

Anchorage photographer Harry M. Walker's spritely look at some of Alaska's most

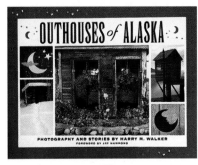

spontaneous architecture has been published as *Outhouses of Alaska*. The book is a delight to hold and behold: Outstanding photographs give readers a glimpse of just how close to nature some Alaskans get. But the book is not just a series of outhouse photos. Gardens, living rooms, crafts, log houses, spectacular scenics and images of Alaskans themselves spring from the pages of this photo-essay gem.

Barrow Alaska from A to Z.

Lyn Kidder. Bonaparte Books, Box 139, 205 East Dimond Blvd., Anchorage, AK 99515. 128 pages, narrow format; 17 b/w photos, 2 maps; softcover, $11.45 includes shipping.

Visitors to Alaska's northernmost community will make the most of their trip by reviewing this handy guide that includes tidbits on just about any subject that could come up about Barrow. From *Aarigaa*, the Inupiaq word for "good" to Zero, where information on the coldest temperature is filed, the text covers an assortment of facts. A sampling includes *Ingutuq*, the Inupiaq name for a young bowhead whale; Lonely, the Distance Early Warning site at Pitt Point; National Bank of Alaska, the largest bank in the state with a branch in Barrow; and Tabasco, whose connection to Barrow is an interesting account of a member of the McIlhenny family, first producers of the famous hot sauce.

—*Penny Rennick*

Statement of Ownership, Management and Circulation

ALASKA GEOGRAPHIC® is a quarterly publication, home office at P.O. Box 93370, Anchorage AK 99509. Editor is Penny Rennick. Publisher and owner is The Alaska Geographic Society, a non-profit Alaska organization, P.O. Box 93370, Anchorage, AK 99509. *ALASKA GEOGRAPHIC*® has a membership of 6,041.

Total number of copies		**15,078**
Paid and/or requested circulation		
Sales through dealers, etc.	0	
Mail subscription	6,041	
Total paid and/or requested circulation	6,041	
Free distribution	0	
Total distribution	6,041	
Copies not distributed (office, use, returns, etc.)	9,037	
Total		**15,078**

I certify that the statement above is correct and complete.

—**Linda Flowers, Circulation/Database Manager**

Index

Photographers

ALASKA GEOGRAPHIC. Back Issues

The North Slope, Vol. 1, No. 1. Out of print.
One Man's Wilderness, Vol. 1, No. 2. Out of print.
Admiralty...Island in Contention, Vol. 1, No. 3. $19.95.
Fisheries of the North Pacific, Vol. 1, No. 4. Out of print.
Alaska-Yukon Wild Flowers, Vol. 2, No. 1. Out of print.
Richard Harrington's Yukon, Vol. 2, No. 2. Out of print.
Prince William Sound, Vol. 2, No. 3. Out of print.
Yakutat: The Turbulent Crescent, Vol. 2, No. 4. Out of print.
Glacier Bay: Old Ice, New Land, Vol. 3, No. 1. Out of print.
The Land: Eye of the Storm, Vol. 3, No. 2. Out of print.
Richard Harrington's Antarctic, Vol. 3, No. 3. $19.95.
The Silver Years, Vol. 3, No. 4. $19.95.
Alaska's Volcanoes, Vol. 4, No. 1. Out of print.
The Brooks Range, Vol. 4, No. 2. Out of print.
Kodiak: Island of Change, Vol. 4, No. 3. Out of print.
Wilderness Proposals, Vol. 4, No. 4. Out of print.
Cook Inlet Country, Vol. 5, No. 1. Out of print.
Southeast: Alaska's Panhandle, Vol. 5, No. 2. Out of print.
Bristol Bay Basin, Vol. 5, No. 3. Out of print.
Alaska Whales and Whaling, Vol. 5, No. 4. $19.95.
Yukon-Kuskokwim Delta, Vol. 6, No. 1. Out of print.
Aurora Borealis, Vol. 6, No. 2. $19.95.
Alaska's Native People, Vol. 6, No. 3. $24.95.
 LIMITED SUPPLY
The Stikine River, Vol. 6, No. 4. $19.95.
Alaska's Great Interior, Vol. 7, No. 1. $19.95.
Photographic Geography of Alaska, Vol. 7, No. 2. Out of print.
The Aleutians, Vol. 7, No. 3. Out of print.
Klondike Lost, Vol. 7, No. 4. Out of print.
Wrangell-Saint Elias, Vol. 8, No. 1. Out of print.
Alaska Mammals, Vol. 8, No. 2. Out of print.
The Kotzebue Basin, Vol. 8, No. 3. Out of print.
Alaska National Interest Lands, Vol. 8, No. 4. $19.95.
Alaska's Glaciers, Vol. 9, No. 1. Revised 1993. $19.95.
Sitka and Its Ocean/Island World, Vol. 9, No. 2. Out of print.
Islands of the Seals: The Pribilofs, Vol. 9, No. 3. $19.95.
Alaska's Oil/Gas & Minerals Industry, Vol. 9, No. 4. $19.95.
Adventure Roads North, Vol. 10, No. 1. $19.95.
Anchorage and the Cook Inlet Basin, Vol. 10, No. 2. $19.95.
Alaska's Salmon Fisheries, Vol. 10, No. 3. $19.95.
Up the Koyukuk, Vol. 10, No. 4. $19.95.

Nome: City of the Golden Beaches, Vol. 11, No. 1. $19.95.
Alaska's Farms and Gardens, Vol. 11, No. 2. $19.95.
Chilkat River Valley, Vol. 11, No. 3. $19.95.
Alaska Steam, Vol. 11, No. 4. $19.95.
Northwest Territories, Vol. 12, No. 1. $19.95.
Alaska's Forest Resources, Vol. 12, No. 2. $19.95.
Alaska Native Arts and Crafts, Vol. 12, No. 3. $24.95.
Our Arctic Year, Vol. 12, No. 4. $19.95.
Where Mountains Meet the Sea, Vol. 13, No. 1. $19.95.
Backcountry Alaska, Vol. 13, No. 2. $19.95.
British Columbia's Coast, Vol. 13, No. 3. $19.95.
Lake Clark/Lake Iliamna, Vol. 13, No. 4. Out of print.
Dogs of the North, Vol. 14, No. 1. $19.95. LIMITED SUPPLY
South/Southeast Alaska, Vol. 14, No. 2. Out of print.
Alaska's Seward Peninsula, Vol. 14, No. 3. $19.95.
The Upper Yukon Basin, Vol. 14, No. 4. $19.95.
Glacier Bay: Icy Wilderness, Vol. 15, No. 1. Out of print.
Dawson City, Vol. 15, No. 2. $19.95.
Denali, Vol. 15, No. 3. $19.95.
The Kuskokwim River, Vol. 15, No. 4. $19.95.
Katmai Country, Vol. 16, No. 1. $19.95.
North Slope Now, Vol. 16, No. 2. $19.95.
The Tanana Basin, Vol. 16, No. 3. $19.95.
The Copper Trail, Vol. 16, No. 4. $19.95.
The Nushagak Basin, Vol. 17, No. 1. $19.95.
Juneau, Vol. 17, No. 2. Out of print.
The Middle Yukon River, Vol. 17, No. 3. $19.95.
The Lower Yukon River, Vol. 17, No. 4. $19.95.
Alaska's Weather, Vol. 18, No. 1. $19.95.
Alaska's Volcanoes, Vol. 18, No. 2. $19.95.
Admiralty Island: Fortress of Bears, Vol. 18, No. 3. $19.95.
 LIMITED SUPPLY
Unalaska/Dutch Harbor, Vol. 18, No. 4. $19.95.
Skagway: A Legacy of Gold, Vol. 19, No. 1. $19.95.
ALASKA: The Great Land, Vol. 19, No. 2. $19.95.
Kodiak, Vol. 19, No. 3. $19.95.
Alaska's Railroads, Vol. 19, No. 4. $19.95.
Prince William Sound, Vol. 20, No. 1. $19.95.
Southeast Alaska, Vol. 20, No. 2. $19.95.
Arctic National Wildlife Refuge, Vol. 20, No. 3. $19.95.
Alaska's Bears, Vol. 20, No. 4. $19.95.

The Alaska Peninsula, Vol. 21, No. 1. $19.95.
The Kenai Peninsula, Vol. 21, No. 2. $19.95.
People of Alaska, Vol. 21, No. 3. $19.95.
Prehistoric Alaska, Vol. 21, No. 4. $19.95.
Fairbanks, Vol. 22, No. 1. $19.95.
The Aleutian Islands, Vol. 22, No. 2. $19.95.
Rich Earth: Alaska's Mineral Industry, Vol. 22, No. 3. $19.95.
World War II in Alaska, Vol. 22, No. 4. $19.95.
Anchorage, Vol. 23, No. 1. $21.95.
Native Cultures in Alaska, Vol. 23, No. 2. $19.95.

PRICES AND AVAILABILITY SUBJECT TO CHANGE

Membership in The Alaska Geographic Society includes four subsequent issues of *ALASKA GEOGRAPHIC*®, the Society's colorful, award-winning quarterly.

Call or write for membership rates or to request a free catalog. *ALASKA GEOGRAPHIC*® back issues are also available (see above list). NOTE: This list was current in late 1996. If more than a year or two have elapsed since that time, please contact us to check prices and availability of back issues.

When ordering back issues please add $2 postage/ handling per book for Book Rate; $4 each for Priority Mail. Inquire for non-U.S. postage rates. To order send check or money order (U.S. funds only) or VISA/MasterCard information (including expiration date and phone number) with list of titles desired to:

ALASKA GEOGRAPHIC.
P.O. Box 93370 • Anchorage, AK 99509-3370
Phone: (907) 562-0164 • Fax (907) 562-0479
e-mail: akgeo@anc.ak.net

NEXT ISSUE:

Moose, Caribou and Muskoxen

Vol. 23, No. 4. Among Alaska's many species of hooved mammals are three species that have come to symbolize the Great Land. This issue takes an in-depth look at the state's moose, caribou and muskoxen, including the latest research on the species. Full-color photos depict the lifestyle and the occasional antics that make these animals such captivating critters. To members early 1997. $19.95.